"OUR BOYS"
Ware Men in the
First World War

Derek Armes

"OUR BOYS"
Ware Men in the
First World War

The Rockingham Press
in association with the
Ware Museum

First published 1998
by The Rockingham Press
11 Musley Lane,
Ware, Herts SG12 7EN

**A catalogue record of this book is available
from the British Library**

ISBN 1 873468 64 4

Printed in Great Britain by
Biddles Limited
Guildford

CONTENTS

ILLUSTRATIONS AND MAPS

INTRODUCTION

The war of 1914-1918 was *the* defining event of the twentieth century. It swept away empires and the carefree way of life of Europe's ruling classes. It created new states throughout Central Europe and the Balkans. It created the conditions for Communism and Fascism. And the peace that followed sowed the seeds of another world war in 1939. The events of eighty years ago are not so distant when one recalls that the immediate cause of the First World War was the assassination of the Austrian Archduke Ferdinand in Sarajevo – a city at the centre of world concern in the nineteen-nineties. On a human level, the 1914-18 war caused the deaths of millions of young men, wiping out almost a whole generation in France, Germany and Britain.

The terrible slaughter of that war still reverberates throughout the towns and villages of Britain. In the small Hertfordshire town of Ware, some 650 men either volunteered or were conscripted later and *at least* 220 of these were killed – *at least* because there are 212 names on the Ware War Memorial and Derek Armes has found others. That represents the horrifying figure of one death for every three Ware men in uniform. Most of these men were in the Hertfordshire Regiment. All those who went to France in 1914 were Herts Territorials and the majority of those who joined later did their training with the Herts, though they may have ended up in other units. Almost every family in Ware lost a son, husband or other relative; every street was affected by the deaths of neighbours. Three women in the town lost four members of their families.

The memories of those events lives on. This book would not have been possible without the generous – and enthusiastic – help of Ware people who treasured the memories, photographs, medals and documents of relatives among "Our Boys" who went from Ware to fight for their country.

This is an important book and I am proud to pay tribute to its author. Derek Armes spent most of his life as a construction engineer and came to historical research by way of family history. For the past three years, he has been a volunteer at the Ware Museum, carrying out the sometimes boring but always important work of accessioning items into the Collection. The many months he has spent on research at the Hertford Record Office, the Public Records Office at Kew and elsewhere have produced a fascinating and very human story. I warmly commend Derek's book to his readers.

David Perman
Hon. Secretary, Ware Museum Trust

Chapter 1
THE PRE-WARE TERRITORIAL ARMY

The 1st Battalion of the Hertfordshire Regiment (Territorial Force) was formed by the amalgamation of the 1st and 2nd Volunteer Battalions of the Bedfordshire Regiment in 1908 with an establishment of 29 Officers and 869 Other Ranks. The battalion was presented with their colours at Windsor by King George V on the 19th June 1909. "C" and "D" Companies of the 1st Volunteer Battalion formed "C" Company of the new Hertfordshire Regiment and comprised detachments from Bishops Stortford, Sawbridgeworth, Ware, Widford, the Hadhams and Braughing. Those members of the new "C" Company from Ware formed a "half Company" and were based at the Drill Hall in Amwell End as were the Regiment's Corps of Drums.

The strength of the Ware half company was sixty-six men including members of the "Drums". The unit was always popular and vacancies to serve in it were few and far between, only becoming available when a man had completed his term of engagement and did not rejoin the colours. Amongst the Ware Territorials were several "old soldiers" who had served in the South African War. Parades were held on Tuesday and Thursday evenings at the Drill Hall. Regular rifle shooting matches took place as well as an annual camp.

The battalion's first annual camp was held in August 1908 at Worthing, the photograph of the group included within the text shows the troops wearing the cap badge of the 1st (Herts) Volunteer Battalion of the Bedfordshire Regiment. When the "Herts Terriers" were formed in 1908 they were issued with "T Herts" shoulder badges but due to a dispute they retained the 1st Volunteer's cap badge for a while – this dates the photograph accurately.

The "Drums" practised on Monday evenings under the direction of their Drum Major, Colour Sergeant E W Abbot of Raynsford Road. Abbot was an "Old Soldier" who had served with the Grenadier Guards in the South African War. The drums are now at the Imperial War Museum at Duxford but until a few years ago they were on display at the Drill Hall. Construction of the Drill Hall was started in 1899, it was built by Simpsons of Marylebone at a cost of £5200 and paid for by Mr E S Hanbury of Poles (now Hanbury Manor). Apart from the main hall it contained an armoury and living accommodation for the Sergeant Instructor. The hall, which is now owned by East Herts District Council, was also used by other organisations in the town.

Men of C Company of the 1st Battalion Hertford Regiment (Volunteer Force) at their first annual camp in 1908 at Worthing. Bill Presland is the soldier standing on the far right. Below: the funeral cortege of Drummer Elthelbert "Burt" Newton with both the Drum and Fife and Regimental Bands in attendance marching to St Mary's Church, Ware in March 1914.

Chapter 2
THE OUTBREAK OF WAR

The storm-clouds of the First World War were gathering throughout the summer of 1914.   Archduke Ferdinand and his wife were assassinated in Sarajevo on the 28th June and exactly a month later on the 28th July Austria declared war on Serbia. From then onwards, war between Europe's two alliances was inevitable.   On the 1st August, Germany declared war on Russia which had been mobilising its army in defence of its ally Serbia.   Two days later, Germany declared war on Russia's ally France and invaded Belgium in an attempt to outflank French defences and reach Paris.   The next day, the 4th August France's ally Britain declared war on Germany.

At the outbreak of war the Hertfordshire Territorials were at their annual camp at Ashridge Park together with their companions in the 162nd East Midlands Brigade – the 1st Battalion Cambridgeshire Regiment, the 5th Battalion Bedfordshire Regiment and the 4th Battalion Northamptonshire Regiment.   They had been there a week when at the crack of dawn on Sunday morning they were awoken by a sergeant banging on the tents and bellowing out "show a leg and strike camp, war has been declared".   Within two hours they were returning to their homes.   Orders for mobilisation were received on Tuesday evening, the 4th August, when war was declared on Germany.

The town of Ware was in a state of ferment during Tuesday and Wednesday from the moment the mobilisation order was issued.   The mood in the town was described in the *Hertfordshire Mercury*:

> The Territorials were seen hurrying hither and thither saying good-bye to their friends and relatives before leaving the town, the reserve men were busy making preparation for active duty in the ranks, the streets were thronged with people anxious to hear the latest news from the seat of operations, and what the latest orders were to be.   Later on in the evening patriotic songs were to be heard from the young bloods of the Territorials and their immediate friends and companions, so for hours the martial element was abroad, and in not a few cases anxiety was writ large on the faces of wives and sweethearts.
>
> Early on Wednesday morning the town presented a very animated appearance, and for two hours large numbers made their way to the Drill Hall, where the members of "C" Company were assembling.   Shortly before nine o'clock, Captain Henry Page Croft of Fanhams Hall, the Commanding Officer, mounted on a splendid charger came on the scene, and, having given instructions preceded the

men to Hertford. The Drum and Fife Band struck up a lively selection, and the men, showing evidence of being ready for any contingency, marched to the railway station, there to entrain for the military barracks at the county town to await further instructions.

At Hertford the Regiment's colours were hung in St Andrew's Church before the troops entrained for Romford two days later *en route* for Bury St Edmunds. "C" Company left Ware in style. One of the Ware barges, owned by the Skipp family, was renamed "Our Boys" and the troops boarded the barge to commence their journey to Romford. How far they travelled by barge is unknown, possibly they went to Hertford to rejoin the rest of the battalion.

Shortly after this all ranks were asked to vary their terms of service which were for home service only to include service overseas in any theatre of war. Some eighty percent of the "Terriers" agreed to serve abroad. The men from Ware were not slow in coming forward with some fifty men prepared to go into action.

Colour Sergeant George Hart compiled the list of the Ware "volunteers" – the reason for that word being in inverted commas will become clear in due course! George Hart had joined "D" Company of the 1st Volunteer Battalion of the Bedfordshire Regiment in about 1885 and transferred to the "Herts Terriers" in 1908. He was a crack shot winning twelve silver spoons inscribed with either "D" Company or "Herts Regt Ware" and bearing hallmarks between 1891 and 1908; he also won a large cup with a marksman on its lid, the lower part of which was eventually given to Ware Football Club as a trophy. His brother was Joseph Hart, the Captain of the Ware Fire Brigade and landlord of the Prince of Wales public house in Crib Street. One of Joseph's sons was William, a plumber by trade and drummer in the "Terriers". When William Hart went to volunteer for overseas service, he found that his uncle George already had him heading the list. William's brother, Joseph Richard Hart, was a regular sailor in the Royal Navy serving mainly in cruisers during the war.

On Friday, the 27th August Lord Hampden, the Commanding Officer of the Hertfordshire Territorial Regiment, officially announced that the Regiment had volunteered for foreign service and that a few vacancies were still open for picked men who should apply at Hertford Drill Hall. Among the volunteers were men such as Ernest Crook, George Presland, Joseph Stamp, Ernest Blows and James Skinner all of whom had served out their time in the "Terriers". Other "time served" Territorials such as L/Corporal J Akers, Private F Game and Drummers S H Clare, S Cadmore and F Blows rejoined the colours later.

Those men who volunteered for overseas service formed the 1st Battalion of the Hertfordshire Regiment while those who elected to remain at home were posted to the 2/1st Battalion. Major H Baker returned from Bury St Edmunds at the end of the month to organise the body of recruits and left on Thursday, the 1st September,

Ware men of C Company marching from the High Street to Bridgefoot in August 1914; and below embarking on a Ware barge, renamed "Our Boys" beside Viaduct Road.

with 104 men. About a third of these volunteers came from Ware including Private "Buff" Robinson of New Road, the first man in the Regiment to be killed on active service.

Meanwhile military activity continued in and around Ware. On Friday, the 21st August, over a 1000 troops of the Royal Berkshire Regiment camped in Ware and Hoddesdon. A rifle range existed in Kibes Lane with a 25 yard covered section and a 50 yard open air range. It was announced that service rifles had been adapted to a small bore with ammunition available at a nominal charge and that there was the opportunity for everyone to learn how to fire a rifle.

Letters and accounts from members of the battalion, printed in the *Hertfordshire Mercury*, describe their activities after leaving Hertford and make interesting reading. One from an unnamed man who was home on a couple of days leave five weeks after leaving Hertford was published on the 19th September and said:

From Hertford we went on to Romford by train, and remained there for ten days. We then left Romford in marching order for Long Melford. We did 18 miles the first day, 13 miles the second day, and a twelve mile march brought us to Long Melford on the third day. We rested for five days, and then went on to Bury St Edmunds, a distance of nine or ten miles. We were billeted in some old maltings about a mile to the east of Bury St Edmunds, but we did not like these old buildings, and so, as the weather was fine, we soon moved out, and have since bivouacked in a field near by. The people have been kindness itself to us while on the march, and would give us anything they had in the way of butter, cheese and so on. The boys have been wonderfully well all the time, the only complaint has been blistered feet. I know some have complained of the food supply. For service conditions it has been remarkably good, but to a man used to luxuries it would be a hardship. For breakfast we have had ham and beef; certainly the ham is rather fat. There has been boiled beef for dinner and potatoes (when we could get them). The bread has been very good. For tea we have had bread and jam, and sometimes butter. Cheese is given out at the same time, and which we are supposed to keep for supper. We have had drills, route marches and so on since we have been here, and we are keeping very fit.

Another letter, with an address given as Rougham Green, infers that the maltings were rat infested (as were some of the older maltings in Ware). Others were luckier being housed with civilians in Bury St Edmunds. Private Walter Page of 40 Crib Street was one of these and he was to marry his landlady's daughter. Page had enlisted in 1913 and was to survive the war although he was wounded four times. In 1968 he wrote an article for *Hertfordshire Countryside* in which he describes some of his experiences with the 1st Battalion in France – some of which are included in this book.

Chapter 3
FRANCE

In 1914 it was generally believed that the Territorial regiments of the British Army would need six months training before they left for France. However the "Herts Terriers" were one of few county regiments of Territorials who went to France within three months of the outbreak of war and they were probably the first to come under fire. The battalion started to prepare itself for embarkation in the early days of November. On the 3rd they were issued with new short ·303 rifles. Two trains took nearly 850 men from Bury St Edmunds to Southampton on Thursday evening, the 5th November 1914, including nearly eighty men from Ware. They left for France on *The City of Chester* at around midnight. Their troopship belonged to the Ellerman Shipping Lines of London: it was some 5413 gross tons built in 1910 and was probably a converted cargo vessel. They landed at Le Havre at midday on the 6th and marched three and half miles to No. 2 Rest Camp. Here they were regaled with lurid tales of the conditions at the Front, but finding that they could buy red wine at 9d (4p) per bottle they thought that it could not be such a bad war after all.

Since the 1st Battalion arrived in an active area before the 22nd November 1914 they were entitled to the 1914 Star (erroneously called the "Mons Star") and could proudly call themselves "The Old Contemptibles". The origin of the name comes from a command given by Kaiser Wilhelm to his military commander on the 19th August 1914 which reads as follows: "It is my Royal and Imperial Command that you concentrate your energies for the immediate present upon one single purpose, and that is, that you address all your skill and all the valour of my soldiers to exterminate the treacherous English and walk over General French's contemptible little army". A list of "Our Boys" known to be entitled to this honour is given in Appendix 2.

It was at No. 2 Rest Camp that Private Charles Castle, the husband of Mrs C Castle of West Street, was tragically killed in an accident with a rifle wound in the head, maybe as a result of not being familiar with the new rifle he had been issued with a couple of days before leaving for France. Castle was one of the volunteers to sign up at Hertford at the outbreak of war.

On the 8th November the Herts Terriers were on their way to the Front and entrained in railway cattle trucks for St Omer. After a few days of preliminary training and a mock attack watched by Brigadier Lord Cavan, they boarded a fleet of London buses driven by the Naval Brigade. They travelled all night and alighted at Poperinghe, across the border in Belgium. From there they marched through Ypres coming under shrapnel fire and entered the trenches at Nonne Bossen where they took over from the Oxfordshire Light Infantry on the 14th November. Nonne Bossen was the farthest the Germans had advanced at this stage of the war and it took its name from a large wood in front of the small hamlet of Westhoek, some three miles to the east of Ypres.

Although the battalion had only been in France a couple of weeks they were learning fast. Captain Page Croft discovered that sacks filled with straw kept his feet warm at night, and so he ensured that every man in "C" Company was issued with two sand bags for the same purpose. Any chicken which was seen, regardless of age, quickly ended up as chicken broth. One night Captain Page Croft was dozing in hole in the ground when he felt something soft and wet pressing against his face – he awoke to discover it was an old sow and her litter of piglets. The battalion ate pork the next evening!!

Private Page recorded that it was very cold and wet and they tried to make themselves comfortable as they were dead tired; they dropped off to sleep only to be rudely awakened by the Germans who shelled them with "coal boxes" – 15 inch shells. Their opponents were the Prussian Guard entrenched some 200 yards away.

Medals, ribbons and badges awarded to Ware men.

Top row: the 1914 Star, War and Victory medals belonging to Sergeant William Hart – medals which were always known to veterans as "Pip, Squeak and Wilfred."

Bottom row: the "Old Contemptibles" badge of Sergeant Hart and the Silver War Badge (for those invalided out of the army through wounds) awarded to Private Henry King.

After two days the Herts Terriers were relieved and marched back to kilometre 3 on the Ypres–Menin road where they sheltered in farm buildings. The next morning they were shelled and suffered their first fatal casualty in action when Private "Buff" Philip Robinson of New Road was killed. "Buff" was another volunteer who joined the colours at Hertford just after the war broke out. Meanwhile at home Mrs Henry Page Croft, the Commanding Officer's wife, was organising a Christmas fund to send presents to the lads at the Front.

The battalion returned to the front lines at Zillebeke where they were shelled and lost five men killed and twenty-one wounded – among the wounded were Private Alfred Bennett of 89 Crib Street who was injured in the hand, and Private C J Clark of Red House Road. At the same time Private Crane of 67 Star Street, was reported to be in hospital in France but it is not known whether he was wounded or sick.

On the 20th November the battalion left the lines and marched in the bitterly cold some 18 to 20 miles south away from the defence of Ypres to Meteren via Ouderdon. Here they rested and reorganised since nearly half of the men were suffering frost bite to their feet. It was at Meteren that they joined up with the 4th (Guards) Brigade of the 2nd Infantry Division who were to be their companions for the ensuing months. They were with the élite of the British Army – the Coldstream, Grenadier and Irish Guards. The Brigade was under the command of the Earl of Cavan who had watched their mock attack a few days earlier.

On the home front the Reserve Battalion (the 2nd/1st Battalion) took the place of the 1st Battalion at Bury St Edmunds. They were destined to defend the East Coast and in October 1915 they were renamed the 1st Reserve Battalion of the Hertfordshire Regiment. Towards the end of November 1914 the War Office approved the establishment of a third battalion which had already been raised and had 240 men in training at Burghley Park at Stamford in Lincolnshire. A fourth training battalion was authorised in 1915. From October 1915 Halton Park, near Tring, was to become the regiment's training area.

Back at the Front the 1st Battalion left Meteren on the 22nd December and marched 19 miles to the outskirts of Béthune carrying full kit and wearing newly issued woolly bear jackets. For a considerable part of the march they were accompanied by the Prince of Wales (later the Duke of Windsor) who was visiting the Front. Normally the pace of an army on the move is that of its slowest unit, but not so with the "Herts Terriers". They were made the leading battalion and on arrival at their assembly point outside Béthune a Guards Officer was heard to remark "They call themselves 'Terriers' – I reckon they are bloody Greyhounds" – a name which was to stay with them for a while. While they waited in the darkness for the return of the billeting parties, a voice shouted from the rear of the battalion: "Albert, give us a song". Albert was Private Albert Hawkes of Ware, a well known baritone, and in response he sang "Little Grey Home in the West". This was followed by a deadly silence broken only by intermittent rifle fire in the distance. The song was to remain a favourite with the "Old Contemptibles". We shall hear more of Albert later.

After spending an uncomfortable night on a tobacco factory floor they went into the lines on Christmas Eve at Dead Cow Farm in front of Richebourg where they relieved an Indian Battalion. Christmas Day was a sad one since Private Percy Huggins of Victoria House, Baldock Street, was killed by a German sniper while on sentry duty in a sap (a "sap" was a trench pushed forward from the front line, used among other things to bomb the enemy's front line trench). Huggins was yet another Ware man who volunteered for service and joined up in Hertford in August 1914.

Reports and letters appeared in the *Mercury* in the New Year and these read as follows: "The 1st Herts spent Christmas Day in the trenches having benefited from a month's sojourn in the rest camp. They proceeded to the front line trenches on Christmas Eve remaining there until day break on Boxing Day". One corporal wrote "it was cold and frosty but we managed to get a fire going and keep warm. We were within 300 yards of the enemy trenches and could distinctly see the enemy at work with shovel and spade and could hear them singing Carols". Another report said "the fighting in which the casualties occurred according to the information contained in a letter from the Front says that the point was only 20 yards separated the British and German lines".

The battalion obviously received their Christmas parcels from home since their C.O., Major Henry Page Croft, wrote to the *Mercury* on the 1st January 1915 expressing thanks on behalf of the battalion for the Christmas gifts of "warm clothing to plum puddings, from soup to soap, from handkerchiefs to potted meat and cigarettes, all of which were included in each man's individual present". A corporal from St Albans at a company reunion recalled that they ate cold Christmas pudding in the front lines. In addition to the presents from home the troops also received a tin of cigarettes and chocolate from Queen Mary – the famous tin which is reputed to have saved several lives when carried in the breast pocket and hit by a bullet.

In the New Year the battalion was re-organised into four companies and in line with their companions in the brigade – the Grenadier, Coldstream and Irish Guards – the new companies were numbered 1,2,3 and 4. The original "C" (Bishops Stortford and Ware) and "D" (Watford) companies combined to form No. 3 Company. All other regiments in the British Army continued to use letters to designate their various companies

Throughout January 1915 the Herts Terriers were with the Guards in and out of the front lines at Richebourg and became well aquainted with the Flanders mud. Major Henry Page Croft in his book *Twenty Two Months Under Fire* described the trenches in these words: "We found that what had been trenches were nothing now but rivers, and only a few posts or 'islands' were held in front". He went on to say that one morning a company returning from their "island" via an old communication trench came under fire and reported that two of their members were missing.

One of the two men was Private Walter Page who described the state of the trenches they encountered as follows: "At Richebourg St Vaast we took over trenches standing with three feet of water. It was madness to hold them. We had to tallow our legs and bind sacking round them. A most unpleasant incident occurred, my mate next to me slipped in the water and got stuck in the mud. I crept along and tried to pull him out but I got stuck as well. We had to stop there all day as they could not get to us in daylight but when night came we were rescued. As we had frost bitten feet we were sent down the line but within a few weeks I was back in the trenches at Festubert". Page was rescued by the Irish Guards

Regular reports of the battalion's activities appeared in the *Mercury*, although as the war dragged on and enthusiasm waned these became less frequent. One from the Front described the conditions they found themselves in during January, it reads : "In a country flat, hedgeless and very poorly timbered, the Hertfordshire Territorials are still taking their share of work in the trenches, and although there is still little doing there is no improvement in which their duty is performed (sic the weather). In the meantime lard and grease of almost all descriptions is used for the foot and legs, a great deal of comfort is claimed in the animal fat as a protection against the cold and liquid mud."

Another correspondent wrote: "Presents of all kinds continue to reach the battalion in abundance, and the troops here are evidently both in the mind and hearts of our friends at home. Supplies, and clothing in particular, are on a liberal scale, and no difficulties are put in the way of obtaining them. The authorities have also arranged for the men to have baths and a complete change of underclothing and two pairs of socks, no one can realise how much this forethought is appreciated by the troops" (from other sources it is known that there were mobile baths at the base camps with steam sterilising units to rid underclothing of bugs and lice.)

These unpleasant conditions seem to cause a lull on both sides, for the German guns were silent and during these rest periods time was found for the more congenial pastime of football. Matches between the "Herts Greyhounds", the Coldstream Guards and the R.A.M.C. took place resulting in victories for the "Greyhounds" by 4-3 and 7-1 respectively.

Two more Officers and 195 men of the 1st Reserve Battalion left Stowlangtoft Hall near Bury St Edmunds and landed in France on the 23rd January. They joined up with the 1st Battalion on the 31st January presumably as cover for sickness and in anticipation of casualties in forthcoming actions. Among the Ware men in the draft were Private Arthur Crook, Private George Keene and Private Fred Hart all of whom were to die in action.

At the end of January Lord Hampden returned to England to take charge of a brigade and Henry Page Croft of Fanhams Hall, now a Major, was promoted as the commanding officer of the 1st Battalion although it was some considerable time before he was made a Lieutenant Colonel. At the same time the battalion moved a

The famous Queen Mary's tin – sent to soldiers filled with chocolate and cigarettes – which is reputed to have saved several lives when carried in the breast pocket and hit by a bullet.

few miles south to the rear of Givenchy and Essars ready to go into action

Until the 6th February the battalion had not taken a very active part in the operations but had been holding a post very near the scene of heavy fighting. However, on the 6th the whole brigade went on the attack near the Pont Fix Road. The Irish Guards and Coldstreams were entrusted with the main assault with the Hertfordshire Regiment being in support and at the disposal of the officer commanding the Irish Guards. The battalion was not in the thickest of the fighting but the men had the gruesome job of burying the dead. The following day they found themselves in rather an exposed position and were very heavily shelled. Captain Pawle, the company commander of No. 3 Company, was seriously wounded by shrapnel in the head and eyes. The only known casualties from Ware in the action of the 6th February were Privates James Bennett and Arthur Saunders, both from Star Street, who received shrapnel wounds. Other casualties around this period were Corporal John Riddle who recovered at Warley, also Privates C J Clark of Red House Road and Ernest Crook of Gladstone Road who were taken to hospital in Birmingham.

The Guards were obviously impressed by the battalion in the action on the 6th February since the following was published in the *Mercury* on the 13th March:

High Praise for the Hertfordshires

Colonel Sir C E Longmore, Commanding the Reserve Battalion of the 1st Hertfordshire (TF) has received from Major H Page Croft, commanding the 1st Battalion at the Front, the following message sent by the General Officer Commanding the 2nd Division to the Officer Commanding the 4 (Guards) Brigade:

"The General Officer Commanding has received with unqualified satisfaction your report of the steady soldier like bearing under heavy fire of the 1st Battalion Hertfordshire Regiment (TF), both in support of the attack on February 6 and again during the bombardment on the afternoon of the following day. He will be glad if you will convey to Major Page Croft and the officers, non-commissioned officers and men his appreciation of their action".

From then on the battalion was known as the "Herts Guards". As far as they had participated in this action, the 1st Battalion had performed their work well. There could be no misgivings that they would not acquit themselves when their own hour of trial arrived.

At the end of February the brigade moved into the Reserve Corps at Béthune, moving out occasionally to dig trenches at Givenchy where they were shelled and suffered casualties. For a time in March the battalion moved into the line adjacent to the La Basse Canal and on the evening of the 11th they relieved the 1st Battalion, King's Royal Rifles in the line with two companies one of which must have been No 3 Company, the Ware Company, for on the next day they suffered casualties. Among the injured was Private Richard Cockman of Ware who was wounded on the 12th March and taken to No 2 Stationary Hospital at Boulogne. Others from the town who suffered wounds were Privates F J Whitby, E Long of 54 Bowling Road, who was wounded in the head, and George Slater of Baldock Street (son of Joe Slater of Cross Street) who was badly wounded in the back by falling masonry when a shell hit the battalion's headquarters at "Windy Corner". George had a long spell in hospital at Cambridge recovering.

April saw them back in the line with the Coldstream Guards. The battalion were now mentors in the art of trench warfare for other Territorial regiments recently arrived in France to form the 47th London Division. Two more drafts joined them from England and more men rejoined the battalion from hospital. Not only were there young men from the town joining up for active service, there were also time-served "Old Soldiers" who joined the Volunteer Defence Corps, open to men who were ineligible for the Army – they played an active part by guarding vital installations at home, such as key bridges. One such man was Fred Brazier of 26 High Street, the son of Charles and Mary Brazier of 4 Coronation Road, a 50 year-old lance corporal who died on Christmas Day 1916. A Commonwealth War Graves

The Western Front map showing Dunkirk, Calais, Poperinghe, Ypres, Passchendaele, Menin, Messines, St Omer, Hazelbrouck, Armentières, Lille, Loos, Tournai, Boulogne, River Lys, Neuve Chapelle, Béthune, Festubert, Lens, Mons, Vimy, Douai, Arras, Cambrai, Bapaume, Albert, Amiens, St Quentin, with BELGIUM and FRANCE labelled, River Somme, River Ancre, River Scheldt.

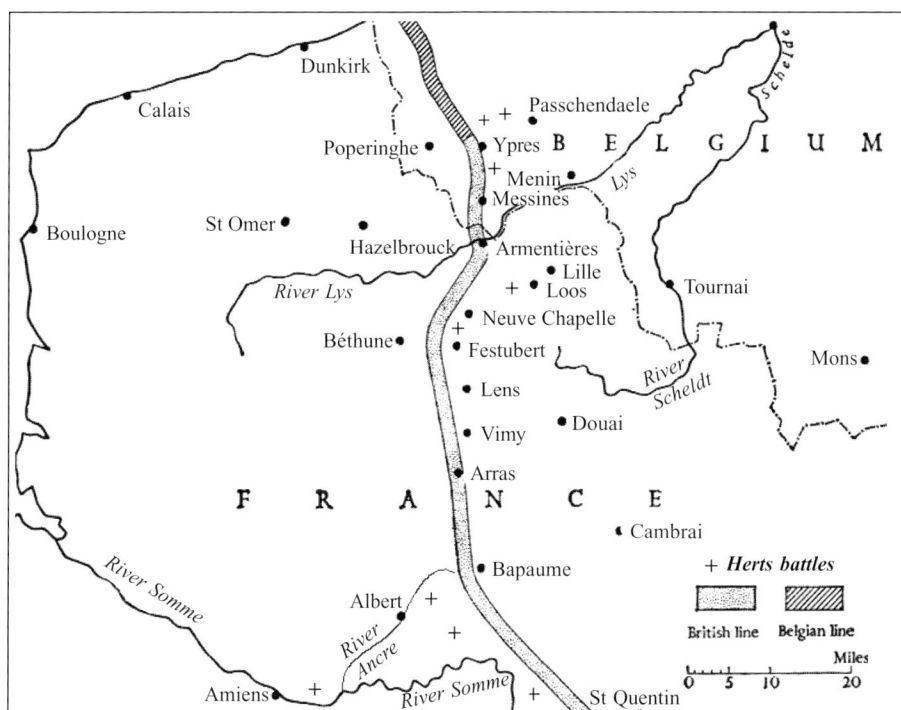

The Western Front and the main battles of the Herts Guards

Commission's headstone in Ware Cemetery marks his final resting place and Fred is also commemorated on the town's War Memorial but the circumstances of his death are unknown. Others joined the Herts Volunteer Regiment whose objective was to encourage recruits who were not of age (or exempt) for the Regular and Territorial Army to learn the basic skills of drill and musketry at an indoor range established at Watton Road.

Other Ware men, who had served in the "Herts Terriers" before the war and emigrated, returned to fight in the regiments of their new countries. Among these were George Hart, the colour-sergeant already mentioned at the outbreak of war, who emigrated to Canada in 1914 after completing 29 years with the Volunteers and Territorials. As a 50 year old he returned to Ware with the Canadian forces. An article in the *Mercury* dated the 4th December 1915 recorded that "Corporal George Hart, of the 60th Canadians, formerly Colour-Sergeant in the 1st Hertfordshires, has arrived in England and is training with his new Battalion in Hampshire. He paid a brief visit to his native town this week and was cordially welcomed by the town's people". Private R Aldridge – formerly of 37 Priory Street – returned with the Canadian Royal Highlanders as did Private J Sullivan with the Canadian Light Infantry. Both were killed in action and their names appear on the Ware War Memorial. Another Ware man who left for Canada in 1907, Sergeant A D Newberry of the Canadian Ordnance Corps, paid a visit to the town while on leave from France.

"Somewhere in France" in 1915 – Private Bill Presland is in the back row second from the left and Ernest Page is fourth from the right.   Below: the whole of C Company with their officers.

Chapter 4
THE BATTLE OF FESTUBERT – MAY 1915

Early in May the battalion moved back into the line at Le Touret in support of the Irish Guards. Although the 1st Battalion had been in the front line with the Coldstream and Irish Guards before, this was the first major battle in which they had "gone over the top" and suffered major casualties. Their hour of trial had arrived.

Sir Douglas Haig had planned an attack against the Aubers Ridge, overlooking the important town of Lille. The attack on the ridge started on Sunday, 9th May, on a front extending from the villages of Bois Grenier to Festubert. The 4th Guards Brigade were in the south and were allotted the section between Rue de Marais and Violaines. The Brigade did not take part in the initial phases of the battle. So from the 13th to the 17th May the the "Herts Guards" bivouacked or stayed in billets at Le Touret. On the 17th they moved up in support of the Irish Guards, some three quarters of a mile to the east of Rue de Lepinette.

At 4.30 am on Tuesday 18th May, the Irish and Grenadier Guards launched their attack with two companies from the 1st Battalion in close support – No 1 Company with the Irish Guards and No 4 with the Grenadiers. As the attack developed the Irish Guards were reinforced by their support company and by additional men from No 3 Company in which the men from Ware served. By 9 am the Irish Guards had secured the first line of trenches and dug in. The Irish suffered very heavy losses and men of the 1st Battalion intermingled with them in the firing line. After this action the Irishmen affectionately called the Herts lads the "Second Micks". All but one of the Irish Guards' officers were killed and for a short time Major Page Croft assumed command, possibly the only time in their history that the Irish Guards were commanded by a Ware man.

A report in the *Mercury* describes how they went over the top, with Major Page Croft leading the charge himself, and how they immediately came under heavy maxim-gun and rifle fire. Their objective was a fortified farm and they got to within 50 yards of it but had to retire, not having enough support to take it. At 9.00pm the battalion took over the line and dug in. All that night and the next day they held the trenches, shells continually dropping and causing heavy casualties. They were relieved on the next day by the 2nd Battalion Coldstream Guards and returned to their billets at La Toure arriving there by 12.30. From here they marched back to Béthune on the following day before going on to Labeuvriere, which Major Henry Page Croft described as "a charming village with many trees all green with early foliage, a brook to bathe in, and woods through which to roam at will and forget".

The words of the common soldiers writing home to their relatives and friends describe the conditions they encountered far better than any historical account of the Battle of Festubert. Extracts of several letters were published in the *Mercury* in June 1915. Private James Fensome writing to a friend at Kimpton says: "I have come out safely from a veritable hell on earth. Oh, how I wish I could forget the sights I saw. It makes my heart bleed to think about it. I dare not tell you all; it was too terrible. You cannot realise in quiet Kimpton what it feels like to stand and see the wounded die because you cannot get at them". Private W Dean of Letchworth said: "We had an experience this week. We were in a battle with the Guards, and it was awful. I was glad when we were relieved for it was murder, not fighting. I thought of 'Home sweet home' many times that day, and there several chaps said prayers, for they sat in trenches wondering when their time was coming. I hope I won't go through any more battles like that". And Corporal H S Woodward of Bishops Stortford wrote: "Our regiment has been in a charge. It was awful. The shells fell thickly, and we had a lot of casualties; we did well and are thought a lot of. It was a piteous sight to see the poor chaps come down wounded, and to see them lying on the battlefield, some dead and others dying. We are fortunately right away from it all".

During the action the battalion lost eight Officers and 18 men killed with 100 men wounded. No men from Ware were killed but several were wounded. The known casualties were :
— Private Joseph Stamp, of 11 Caroline Court, Baldock Street;
— Privates Fred Crook and his brother Arthur of 32 Gladstone Road;
— Privates Samuel and his brother Henry of Bury Field Terrace – both were wounded in the hand;
— Private William Presland of Coronation Road, wounded in the abdomen and taken to hospital at Birkenhead (his brother George was there as well);
— Private Walter E Page of 40 Crib Street, injured in the foot, repatriated to recover in Newcastle;
— Private Frederick Gayler of 97 Star Street, wounded in the hand;
— Private William Jackson of 10 Bowling Road, gassed and wounded by an exploding shell;
— Private Robert Castle of 44 Priory Street;
— Private E W Wallace, wounded in arm, repatriated to Sunderland;
— Private William T Hills of Musley Hill. William (Billy) Hills went to France in the "Drums", it is known that he and his fellow drummer Billy Hart fought in the trenches and so it would appear that the "Ware Drums" did not follow the usual practice of musicians acting as stretcher bearers.

Two servicemen from Ware in the "Herts Guards" were awarded medals in the King's Birthday Honours for 1915. Sergeant-Major Ernest W Abbot, who was the battalion's Drum-Major at the outbreak of war, was awarded the DCM as was Sergeant Francis Rayment (Acting Company Quarter Master Sergeant) a Ware man

English Miles

0	1	2

—————— *Roads*

/////////// *Canal*

• • • • • • • • *British lines*

— — — — — — *German lines*

AUBERS RIDGE

Neuve Chapelle •

Richebourg St Vaast

FESTUBERT

Violaines

BÉTHUNE

La Bassée-Béthune Canal

Givenchy

LA BASSÉE

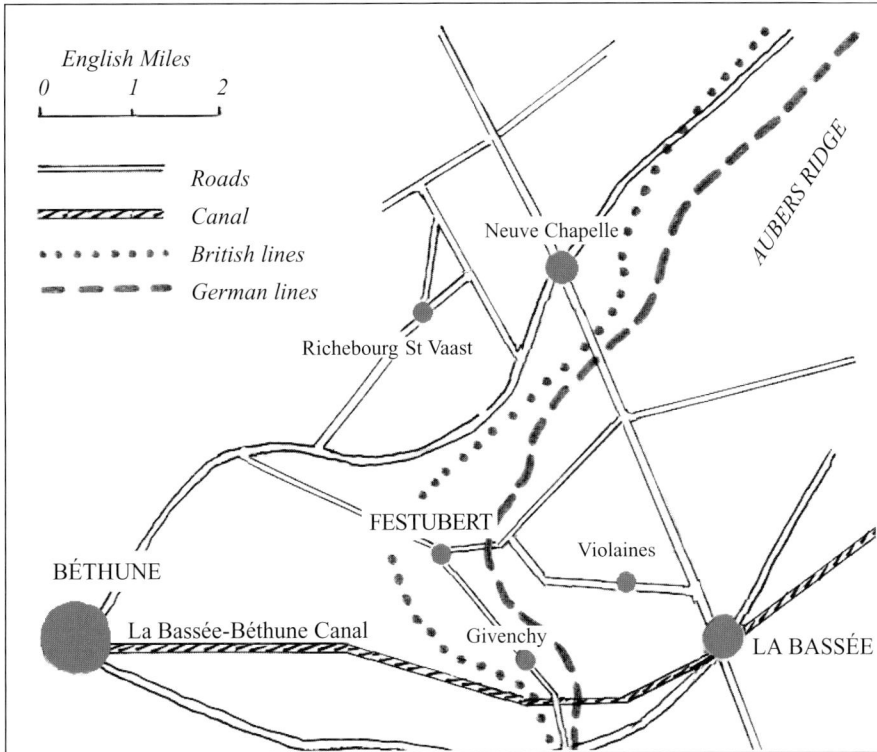

The Battle of Festubert, May 1915

who was a schoolmaster at Boreham Wood at the outbreak of war. Sergeant Rayment was to become a Company Sergeant Major and later an officer cadet receiving his commission on the 4th August 1916. He continued to serve as an officer with the 2/1st Battalion which was unusual since officers promoted from the ranks were normally posted to other regiments.

Following this action several of the men who left for France in November 1914 returned home to Ware for seven days leave. With Sergeants Jackson and Hiram Hammond was Lance Corporal Ben Newton. A local correspondent wrote to the *Mercury* to say that "it was a very amusing and inspiring sight to see Lance Corporal Newton on his way to the station when he returned. With his full war equipment, and a face covered in smiles, he was accompanied by his wife and half a dozen children, and the townspeople turned out and gave him three hearty cheers". Ben and his family lived at 2 Cherry Tree Yard in Amwell End – happily he survived the war, ending his service days at Luton with the 575th Employment Company.

The battalion returned to their billets at Béthune on the 19th May to reform. Throughout June they were in and out of the line with the Grenadier Guards in the vicinity of Vermelles. At the end of June Earl Cavan (a Hertfordshire man) who commanded the 4th Guards Brigade was promoted to command a Division. In his farewell order he said, "We welcomed the 1st Herts Territorials at Ypres, and most worthily have they borne their part with us".

For the next three months until mid August the "Herts Guards" remained in the 4th Brigade and spent spells in the line in the Cuinchy area with breaks at the Montmorcey Barracks. Fresh drafts of men joined the battalion in August. The 15th August saw the 1st Battalion marching back from the Front to billets at Beuvry. On the 19th the Guards left the area and one company of the battalion marched into Béthune to take their farewells of the Coldstreams, Grenadiers and Irish Guards, with whom a strong bond had developed.

The "Herts Guards" now joined the 6th Brigade, still part of the 2nd Division. The 27th August saw them digging a new communication trench from Pont Fix and Windy Corner Road to the junction of Whitehall and Hatfield Road, obviously part of their old lines. On the 4th September they marched to Cambrin, where they were in and out of the line with their new companions the King's Royal Rifles (K.R.R), the 2nd South Staffords, the 2nd Essex and the 17th Middlesex Regiments. The 6th Brigade were relieved on the 30th September, the Herts returned to Béthune on their way to the front line trenches at Vermelles the next day. By the 3rd of September they were back at Béthune where more men were drafted into the 1st Battalion. These men had come from the 3/1st Battalion but had been on attachment to the 4th Entrenching Battalion.

An article in the *Mercury* dated the 4th September records that Mr and Mrs William Lee of 69 Crib Street had four sons serving in the forces. William and Walter with the R.A.M.C, Harry in the Herts Territorials (he was to transfer to the Royal Berkshire Regiment and was killed in April 1918) and Frederick in the Royal Navy. (Another son, Philip Charles, was to join the Royal Berkshires and was killed in action in 1917.)

This report on the Lee family produced swift responses from Mr and Mrs Robert Castle of 44 Priory Street and Mr and Mrs Joe Slater of 5 Cross Street. From their letters in the local paper one can gauge the effect the war had on various streets in the town. Mr and Mrs Castle stated that there were 40 men serving in the forces from Priory Street and that they had four sons in the army – Robert was in the "Herts Guards" and had been wounded at Festubert (he was wounded again in 1916), the others were in the King's Royal Rifles, the 9th Battalion of the Bedfordshires (this was Alban Castle who was to die of wounds received on the 23rd December 1915) and the East Anglia Royal Field Artillery. Mr and Mrs Slater must have held the town's record for the number of sons in the forces, seven in total. Their son George was seriously injured in action with Hertfordshire Regiment in 1915 and later joined the Queen's Regiment. The Slaters were fortunate to only lose one son, Samuel who joined the Bedfordshire Regiment and was subsequently killed with the Lincoln-shire Regiment.Around this time Major Henry Page Croft of Fanhams Hall was promoted to the rank of Lieutenant Colonel.

Chapter 5
THE BATTLE OF LOOS – SEPTEMBER 1915

On the 17th September the battalion moved from Béthune to Gonnechen and a few days later to the Annequin–Cambrin area. Here they shared spells in the line with the King's Royal Rifle Corps and the 2nd Staffs until the end of the year. Their division was on the northern fringe of the action with the main fighting taking place some five miles to the south. During this spell two Ware men were killed in action. Private George Keene, who prior to enlisting worked for the Ware solicitor Mr G H Gisby, was killed n the 26th October by a grenade in a section of the trenches known as "A1". On the 21st November Private John Newton, a 17 year-old lad of 6 Chapel Buildings, Amwell End, was shot through the head while in the trenches north east of Vermelles.

The families of those killed or wounded were notified by the Territorial's Record Office at Warley in Essex – however in most instances letters were also received from either their officers or comrades-in-arms almost immediately. Those who died in the field were normally buried by their comrades in the battle area where they fell with their graves being marked by a simple cross or upturned rifle and helmet. Those who died of wounds were buried in cemeteries established next to the dressing stations, casualty clearing stations and base hospitals to the rear of the Front.

The grave of Sergeant William Miles of Watford of "C" Company (an amalgamation of the old Ware and Watford companies) shown in the photograph on the next page is unusual since it marked with a stone and not the more usual wooden cross. Miles died on the 7th November at the Béthune Base Hospital and his grave is in the town cemetery, the original headstone being replaced with one by the War Graves Commission. Although not a Ware man he was obviously a pal of Drummer Billy Hart of Crib Street (by now a Sergeant) who kept the photo in his service wallet.

Every man going to France made a will disposing of his estate – often this amounted only to his army back pay. This often involved "red tape" as Mrs Presland discovered when her son George was killed in 1916: her initial claim on her son's estate was rejected since she and not her husband had signed the appropriate form. At this time married women had no legal rights to property and her husband was directed to sign the appropriate form (or put his mark) in the presence of the magistrate Mr AH Rogers, who owned the newsagent's shop at the bottom of New Road. When a soldier was killed his family often placed a card in their front window with crossed Union Flags at the top and the soldier's photograph below.

Dependants were looked after by SSFA (Soldiers and Sailors Families Association). Mrs Richard Benyon Croft of Fanhams Hall (the mother of Lieut Col Page Croft) was President of the Ware Division of the Hertfordshire Branch and her daughter Ann Page Croft was the Treasurer and Hon Secretary. The Ware representatives on the committee were Mrs R B Croft and Mrs Pickering. During the year 1914-15 the Association paid out grants of £450-19s-8d to 78 wives, 169 children and 114 "other relatives", the money having been collected by donations.

Many of the town's younger servicemen were former members of the Ware Boy Scouts under the leadership the Curate of St Mary's, the Revd F W Farmer, who wrote and received many letters from former members of the troop. One such letter from George Storey who went to France on the 29th September 1915 with the Lancashire Fusiliers was written from "somewhere in France" on the 20th November 1915. He said that he had seen the Herts Terriers more than once and that he had spoken to several lads from the town, which meant that he was in the Béthune area

The grave of Sergeant W. Miles in Béthune Cemetery was unusual in having a stone cross rather than a wooden one.

of the Front. He went on to say that the predominant feature in the trenches was "mud, mud and more mud" and that "you soon got used to stew for dinner every day and that army rations were composed of bread, cheese, jam, bacon and tea". George was to die of wounds received "at home" and is buried in Ware Cemetery.

Back at home Mrs Henry Page Croft launched another appeal for donations to buy Christmas presents for the boys at the Front. This year Christmas puddings for the whole regiment were sent together with separate packages for each man containing a writing case and prayer book, a handkerchief, chocolate and bull's-eye sweets, potted meat, soup tablets and a cake of soap. This was the last Christmas that Mrs Page Croft organised parcels for the troops at the Front. Early in 1916 a committee was formed to take charge of "The Ware Boys at the Front Fund". Its President was Lieut-Col G R McMullen who lived at Presdales in Hoe Lane, Dr. W G Stewart was its Chairman and Mr T W Jennings the Secretary. Funds were raised through fetes, one such fete held at Presdales on August Bank Holiday Monday raised £158. Initially parcels were sent throughout the year to all servicemen at the Front.

Although the troops acknowledged the parcels and said nice things about them, they were not always a success and sometimes provoked uncomplimentary remarks, for instance when the cigarettes got mixed up with the tomatoes. Another man wrote and said that the sausages were in such a state when they arrived that they put them in the trenches to scare the rats away! The reference to rats may seem funny but they were detested by the troops. One battle hardened veteran from the town related to his relatives that he was carrying two mugs of cocoa through waterlogged trenches littered with dead bodies when he tripped and fell – he broke down and wept when he saw rats scurrying from the corpses. As the war progressed and food controls were imposed at home, food parcels were replaced by postal orders with which the troops could buy little luxuries at such establishments as the YMCA and the Church Army huts.

PUBLIC NOTICES.

CHRISTMAS GIFT FUND,
1ST HERTFORDSHIRE REGIMENT.

Mrs. Henry Page Croft will be very grateful for any donations for the purchasing of

CHRISTMAS GIFTS
for the Regiment, to be sent out to the Front early in December.

Donations may be sent to the Christmas Gift Fund, London County and Westminster Bank, Ware; or to Mrs. Croft, 53 Onslow Gardens, London, S.W.

Chapter 6
1916

From the 27th December until the 15th January the battalion trained at Ham en Artois where two more drafts totalling some 120 men were received from England. On the 16th they marched back to Béthune and the following day into the support area at Givenchy where they settled into the routine of going in and out of the line at Richebourg St Vaast.

War could have its humorous side. Walter Page records that once they came across a pig which had obviously been killed by shell fire. They obtained permission from the company officer to "dispose" of it and "operation carve up" commenced. A search was made to find a chopper or axe and Page or one of his comrades returned with a four-foot tree-felling saw which raised a big laugh. The pig was duly dismembered with the saw, aided by Page's kukri knife, and a tasty meal was cooked in an old iron water butt.

The battalion's commander, Lieut Col Henry Page Croft was promoted to command the 68th Brigade on the 7th February. This was another first for the battalion and for Ware since it is believed that Henry Page Croft was the first Territorial Officer to achieve the rank of Brigadier General (now a Brigadier) and to lead a brigade in France. Command of the 1st Battalion then passed to Major Frank Page, a Hertford man and former Mayor of the county town in 1912 who had served in the Boer War. He won the DSO in June 1915 and was to add a bar to this medal at the Battle of Ancre.

Further spells in the line followed in the Festubert area until the 28th February when the battalion was allotted to the GHQ Troops area. They entrained to Ebblingham and now came under the orders of the 118th Brigade linking up with the 1/6th Cheshires, the 1/1st Cambridgeshires and the 4/5th Black Watch. Following inspections by the "Top Brass" the battalion joined the 39th Division under canvas near Sercus on the 8th March before moving back to the Festubert area via Merville and Pont du Hem. During this period a further 150 men joined them from the 3/1st Battalion.

March and April saw the return of seven of the "Herts Terriers" who went to France in November 1914 and had completed their term of their engagement with the Territorials. Private George Clark arrived home on the 18th March followed on the 6th April by William Hart, now a sergeant, together with Privates William Presland, Ernest Page, Ernest Johnson and Frederick Cox (known as "Treacle"). Hart and Presland had both joined the "Terriers" on the 8th April 1908. Each was granted three weeks leave and given their discharge papers on the 28th April. They were

Brigadier-General Page Croft CMG and (right) his successor as commanding officer of the 1st Battalion Hertfordshire Regiment, Lieut Col Frank Page. Henry Page Croft was born at Fanhams Hall was managing director of the maltsters Henry Page & Co. He took the company to France in November 1914 as a captain and was successively promoted, becoming the first Territorial officer to achieve the rank of Brigadier-General. After the war, he became Conservative MP for Bournemouth and was created Baron Croft in 1939, when he became Under-Secretary of State for War in Churchill's Cabinet. He died in 1947.

quickly followed by Company Sergeant-Major Ernest Abbot DCM on the 17th April who to mark his retirement had been presented with a silver teapot by the officers in his company. The "retirement" of these Herts Terriers provoked adverse comment in the local press, probably from somebody ignorant of the fact that they were placed on the Army Reserve and were liable for recall anyway. They were stoutly defended by Captain Pawle, their company commander. However, for most of them, retirement was not the end of their army service. George Clark rejoined the "Herts Guards" and paid the final sacrifice on the 3rd July 1917. William Hart rejoined the regiment and served with one of the home battalions until 1917 when he went to East Africa with the King's African Rifles. The inseparable pals, Bill Presland and Ernest Page rejoined the army serving with the Royal Horse Artillery, while Ernest Abbot rejoined the Hertfordshire Regiment.

In France, two months in and out of the lines in the Festubert and Givenchy sectors followed before the 1st Battalion was pulled back for a spell of rest and

If this certificate is lost or mislaid no duplicate of it can be obtained.   Army Form E. 511.

DISCHARGE CERTIFICATE OF A SOLDIER OF THE TERRITORIAL FORCE.

This is to certify that (No.) *235* (Rank) *Sgt.*

(Name) *William Charles Hart*

(Unit) HERTFORDSHIRE REG⊤ who was enlisted

to serve in the Territorial Force of the County of *Hertfordshire*

on the *eighth* day of *April* 19 *08,*

* Here state cause of discharge as detailed (a) for peace conditions in the Regulations for the Territorial Force, or (b) during a period of embodiment in para. 392, King's Regns.

is discharged in consequence of * *Termination of period of engagement K.R. 392 xxi* and that his claims have been properly settled.

, His total service in the Territorial Force is *8* years *17* days, including *1* years *266* days embodied service.

Service abroad, viz., in *France*   *1* years *152* days.

Medals, Clasps, and Decorations *Nil*

(Signature of Officer Commanding Unit) *Capt*

(Place and Date) HERTFORD 27 APR 1916 19 .

D, D, & L., London, E.C.   Forms
A3918 Wt.W13547/3024 300,000 12/15 Sob. 62   B, 511
                                          5

William Hart's discharge certificate after completing his engagement with the Hertfordshire Territorials in April 1915. He then rejoined the army.

recuperation at Ferme du Roi near Béthune on the 28th May. Their respite was short lived and they were soon back to the normal trench routine in the Givenchy Sector, including raids on the German trenches for prisoners. It was in this sector that 4302 Private Alfred Smith of Ware was killed on the 10th June 1916.

On the 1st July the battalion was back in the line at Jeunne du Bois where they remained for three days before marching back to the Givenchy-Cuinchy sector. They stayed here until the 24th with both sides raiding each other's trenches but neither gaining any success. It was here that Private W H Taylor was killed on the 23rd July. When the battalion came out of the line they marched back to Goore where they spent a couple of nights before marching on to Béthune and were billeted in a local school, the École des Jeunes Filles. They probably returned to the lines on the 30th July.

Besides the men killed in action it is known through the casualty lists that men from the town were wounded during their spells in the trenches at the Festubert, Givenchy and Vermelles sectors. They were :

— 4298 Private Frederick Mason;

Four Ware men appear in this photograph of C Company, taken in April 1916 and published in the Mercury. Sergeant John Riddle of Cross Street (far left in back row) went to France in 1914: he returned home through illness and did valuable work in obtaining recruits – he returned to France in 1915 and survived the war. Sergeant Hiram Hammond (far left in middle row) was a pre-war Terrier who went to France as a corporal with the original draft: he became the senior sergeant in his company and was killed at the Battle of St Julien in July 1917. Company Sergeant Major Edward Clarke of London Road (middle row second left) was another "Old Contemptible" – he suffered frost bite in the winter of 1915. Quarter Master Sergeant Joseph Ketterer (middle row second right) was another pre-war Terrier: he went to France as a sergeant and ended the war as the battalion's Regimental Quarter Master Sergeant.

— 5402 Private F C Savage (later killed in action with the Bedfordshires);
— 1815 Private F Game;
— 5095 Private A Clark of Maltings Yard, who convalesced at the South African Military Hospital at Richmond;
— 2325 Private Robert Castle of 44 Priory Street was wounded in the eyes and spent time in the 7th General Hospital in France;
— 3322 Private F Hart of 12 Priory Street was wounded in the arm and leg and sent to the 8th Stationary Hospital in France.

On the 10th August the battalion came out of the line and returned to Béthune. The next day they marched at the head of the 118th Brigade on their way to Gustieville by way of Cauchy à la Tour and Mouchy Breton. A typical days march was about fifteen miles. They were destined for "pastures new" on the Somme.

At Gustieville the 1st Battalion undertook a spell of training for some ten days during which Lance Corporal James Akers of 9 New Road was accidentally injured in his foot during bayonet practice. They then marched to Bus Les Artois on the 25th August. Bus Les Artois was alive with huts and tents set in apple and pear orchards and a great ammunition dump had been established in the nearby forest. Here they were billeted in huts before marching to a wood near Englebelmer the next morning where they bivouacked. They had reached the Somme killing fields below the Thiepval heights. Englebelmer lay some four and a half mile north of the town of Albert and a couple of miles or so from the Front. Apart from a staging area it was also used as a Field Ambulance Station.

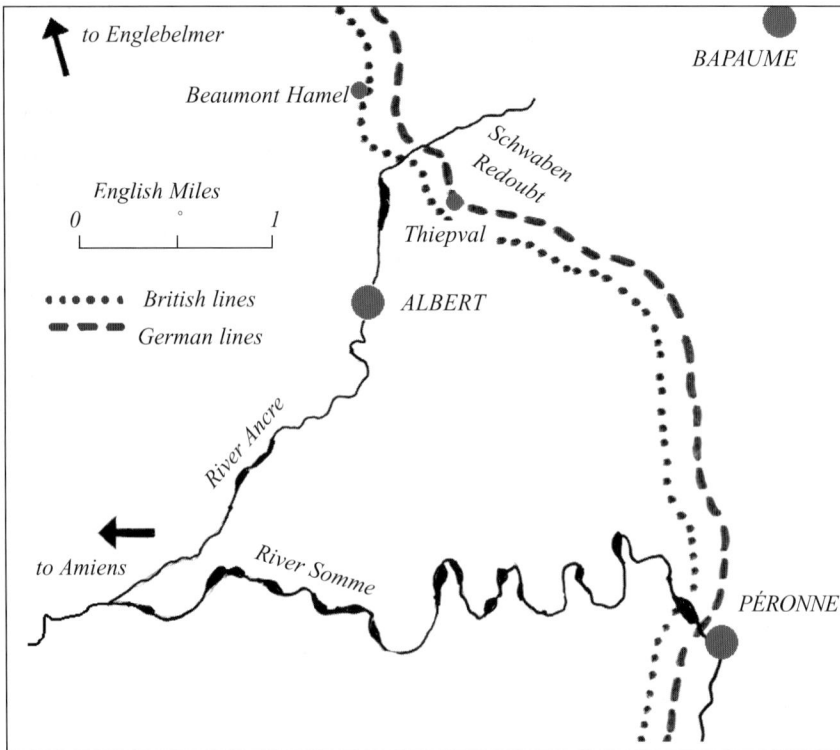

The Battle of Ancre – September to October 1916

Chapter 7
THE BATTLE OF ANCRE – AUTUMN 1916

The Battle of the Somme, scene of the worst slaughter of the war, had been going on relentlessly since the 1st July.   Sir Douglas Haig's intention was to drive a battering ram through the German lines and achieve a "breakthrough".   At this point the Front was to the west of St Quentin, in the upper valley of the River Somme and its tributary the River Ancre.   When the first attack failed to gain any ground at all, though at the cost of 19,000 British dead and 57,000 wounded, Haig kept doggedly on over the following months sending more and more troops against the enemy machine guns.

The 39th Division attacked the enemy's trenches north of the River Ancre on the 3rd September with the 118th Brigade held in reserve.   The attack was a failure and the 118th Brigade took over the original lines in the evening where they were heavily shelled during the night.   The Herts Battalion remained here until the 12th when they were relieved and marched back to Englebelmer.   It was probably during this spell at the Front that Private Charlie French of 46 Bowling Road was wounded.

The 3rd of October saw the battalion back in the lines at Beaumont Hamel which lay in the marshy Ancre Valley, their march from Englebelmer probably being by cross-country tracks over the Downs of Mesnil.   Here they remained until the 7th October when they were relieved by the 11th Sussex, their comrades in the 118th Brigade.   They marched back to billets and bivouacs at Maetinsart.   The camp here was in woods which were also the home of siege howitzers which fired close by day and night.   According to one witness the huts creaked and groaned every time they fired.   Just to add to the troops' discomfort the wood was rat-infested.   The author Edmund Blunden, who served in the 11th Sussex battalion, mentions the wood in his book *The Undertones of War*.   He recalled that they made a circuit through Martinsart Wood on their way up to the Hamel trenches, remarking on the howitzers, the mud and the "confusion" of hutments.

After three days "rest" the 1st Herts Battalion returned to the lines on the right of the Schwaben Redoubt – a large and highly fortified German defence system standing on the top of a hill overlooking the village of Thiepval which had defied complete capture by our troops for weeks.   It was here that 2072 Private Sidney Ditton of Vicarage Road received gunshot wounds to his knee on the 13th October (he recuperated later at Eastbourne).   On the afternoon of the 14th the 118th Brigade attacked the Redoubt, the Cambridgeshires and the Black Watch taking the remainder of it.   The 1st Herts Battalion sent one platoon as reinforcements but were not otherwise involved, except for being heavily shelled.   They were to remain here for a couple of days before being pulled out of the line.

They marched back to billets at Englebelmer and then on to Senlis north of Henecourt which was used as a camp by the infantry. Again Edmund Blunden refers in his book to the barns and *estaminets* (cafés and bars) of Senlis. Here the Herts Battalion relaxed for eleven days before returning for further spells in the lines at Schwaben Redoubt where Private Edward Smith of 145 Musley Hill was killed on the 30th October. When not in the line they were in the dug-outs at Authuille. This was another spot known to Edmund Blunden who wrote that his battalion were billeted in Authuille built against the high bank called The Bluff and there passed some pleasant hours. In another section of his book he wrote "we rested in cabins like dugouts called Authuille Bluffs, on the steep rise from the Ancre inundations".

The battalion left the Front on the 3rd November and marched to Pioneer Road where they received more drafts from the 3rd Battalion. It was not long before the battalion and its new men were in action again. During the evening of the 12th November the battalion left Pioneer Road and marched in light fighting order to the Schwaben Redoubt where it formed up in four lines at 5.45am on the 13th. Just before dawn broke and in thick mist the guns opened fire and the battalion went forward, the Cambridgeshires on their left and the East Lancashires (from the 19th Division) on their right. Direction was kept and the battalion had very soon taken all its objectives, capturing the whole of the Hassa line and advancing to a depth of 1600 yards, killing many Germans and capturing some 250 prisoners. The new line was consolidated and the battalion held the new position till the night of the 13th/14th. During the period the Germans made three raids against a bombing post on the left of their line but these were successfully driven off. The battalion were relieved during the night of the 14th/15th November and marched back to huts at Aveluy on the west side of the River Ancre.

Number 3 Company in which most of the Ware men served was in the thick of the action and showed considerable gallantry. Of the 15 Military Medals won by the battalion four – together with a Distinguished Conduct Medal – were awarded to "Our Boys". The original citations for the Military Medal no longer exist, however the Anglian Regiment's Museum at Duxford holds notes from an unknown source which gives details of the awards made at Ancre. The following relate to "Our Boys":

— 2865 Corporal George Reynolds of London Road won his Military Medal when he assisted Lieutenant Smallwood in collecting men from all units and organised them so that they could be led forward to the final objective, the Mill Trench, which they captured and consolidated. He showed great initiative and great judgement in recognising what needed doing. He also volunteered to cross the River Ancre with Lieutenant Johnson to reconnoitre the Mill which was supposed to be a strong point. Lieutenant Smallwood, a London man, received the Military Cross.

— 2567 Private Claud Sweeney, also of London Road, and 2291 Private Richard Page of Bowling Road were awarded the Military Medal for gallantry. They

Private Henry King (right) photographed with a pal. The photograph was taken before November 1916 when Henry was badly wounded in the Ancre battle on the Somme. He came back to England to recover and was due for discharge. However, against the wishes of his family, he reported back to his unit and joined the newly formed 2nd Garrison Battalion of the Bedfordshire Regiment. In March 1917 the battalion went to India where Henry contracted malaria. He was discharged from the army through ill health with a "Silver War Badge" in July 1919, and resumed work at Allen and Hanbury.

bombed a dugout and when three German officers and 29 men came up from it armed, the two Ware men disarmed and captured them. When their platoon corporal, Ernest Jackson of Kibes Lane, was mortally wounded Private Page took command of the bombing post at Point 35. Both he and Private Sweeney were conspicuous in assisting in the capture of the German machine gunners.

— 4549 Private John Gray, also of Bowling Road, won his Distinguished Conduct Medal while escorting a party of prisoners from the Front – one wonders if they were some of those captured by Claud Sweeney and Richard Page. Private Gray was sent back with one other man to escort a batch of prisoners consisting of an officer and 14 men. The German officer who had managed to hide his revolver shot the guard and would doubtless have done more damage had not Gray rushed on him and killed him with the butt of his rifle. Having shot another prisoner and thus enforced order, Gray brought the remainder back safely. The unfortunate guard shot by the German Officer was Private Charles Martin of Princes Street, Ware.

— 3322 Private Frederick Hart of Priory Street won his Military Medal repelling a German counter attack. He did excellent work by his bomb throwing on the occasion of a hostile attack on the 14th November, but was blown out of the trench by a bomb explosion and lay there unconscious until found after the attack had been driven off. Corporal Joseph Stamp of Caroline Court was probably killed at the same post.

Of the above medalists only Richard Page was to survive the war.

Another Ware man, 4345 Private William (Bill) King of Scotts Road, was mentioned in despatches. Bill may have been wounded since he was transferred to the Lincolnshire Regiment with whom he was captured on the 31st July 1917 and spent the remainder of the war as a POW at Münster. His brothers 2510 Private Alfred King and 2736 Private Henry King served in the Herts Regiment. Alf was to transferred to the 4th Battalion of the Gloucestershires, while Henry was transferred to the 2nd Garrison Battalion of the Bedfordshires and posted to India.

The price paid by the battalion during this attack was high. Seven officers were wounded, 20 other ranks were killed with a further five missing. One hundred and fifteen men were wounded. Ware grieved after this battle, six men from the town paid the supreme sacrifice with many more injured. Those killed in this action or subsequently died of their wounds were:
— 3156 Acting Corporal Frank Gray of 11 Gladstone Road;
— 4785 Private Walter Andrews of 8 Prices Street died of wounds;
— 2273 Private Joseph Clibbon of 1 Francis Street, reported missing and subsequently confirmed that he had been killed (he had been wounded earlier in the year);
— 2276 Lance Corporal Ernest Jackson of 3 Kibes Lane died of his wounds on the 17th November;
— 4593 Private Charles Martin of Princes Street;
— 2528 Cpl Joseph Stamp of 11 Caroline Court, Baldock Street;
— 266276 Private Ernest Warley of 169 Musley Hill.

Among the many men from the 1st Battalion wounded in the battle it is known that the following were from Ware:
— 2070 Private E Long of 54 Bowling Road received gunshot wounds in his left thigh and convalesced at Nottingham (he had been previously wounded in 1915);
— 2677 Lance Corporal E Andrews;
— 2854 Lance Corporal W Middleton;
— 2583 Private Arthur Smith of Century Road;
— 2544 Private D Waller;
— 3280 Lance Sergeant George Adams received shrapnel wounds and was taken to the Fletcher Convalescent Home at Cromer. Before he joined up he worked at Harvey's store in Ware;
— 4125 Private Ablet;
— 2723 Private Alfred Baker;
— 3283 Private George A Bently of 2 Blue Coat Yard;

Wounded soldiers recuperating in Ware Priory which became a VAD hospital. Seated centre is Dr W G Stewart, Medical Director. Right: the plaque on the wall of the Priory which commemorates its use as a hospital "during the Great War".

THE · BRITISH · RED · CROSS · SOCIETY
AND · THE · ORDER · OF · SAINT · JOHN
GRATEFULLY · ACKNOWLEDGE · THAT
THIS · BUILDING · WAS · CONVERTED · AND
USED · AS · AN · AUXILIARY · HOSPITAL
WORKED · BY · A · VOLUNTARY · STAFF
DURING · THE · GREAT · WAR

— 2753 Private Samuel Campkin of Buryfield Terrace;
— 4549 Private John Gray of 22 Bowling Road (killed in 1918);
— 5617 Private C W Philpot;
— 4193 Sergeant Arthur H Wilbourne (killed in 1918);
— 3329 Private W Devonshire of Musley Lane wounded in eye, leg and arm, taken to hospital in Birmingham;
— 1833 Private S Goody;
— 5048 Private Solomon Trundle of 7 Church Alley;
— 5702 Private Robert Skipp of 61 New Road;
— 2736 Private Henry T King, recovered at Aldershot.

Many servicemen were brought back home to Ware to convalesce and recuperate. Mrs Croft, of Fanhams Hall which she had rebuilt as a stately home, had bought the Priory in 1913 and eventually gave it to the town. In 1914 she allowed the Priory to be used as a VAD (Voluntary Aid Detachment) convalescent hospital. A local doctor, Dr W G Stewart, was the Medical Director and his wife held the post of matron. Although it is not known if any Ware men from the Herts Regiment stayed there, one Ware man certainly did. He was Petty Officer Simpson who was seriously injured at Beaucourt sur l'Ancre in November 1916, serving with the 63rd Naval

Division which fought in close proximity to the "Herts Guards". Simpson won the DCM in this action and was presented with his medal at the Priory. The use of the Priory as a convalescent hospital is commemorated by a plaque adjacent to the main entrance doorway.

The nurses and other helpers were young women from Ware and district – Among a list Hertfordshire ladies whose names were recorded for their valuable services with the Red Cross was a Miss Spicer for VAD work in Ware. One assumes it was for fund raising or similar work. One of the cooks at the Priory was Edith Hitch who later married Major T C Hunt and, as Edith Hunt, became the town's historian.

Trained men from the 2nd and 3rd Battalions had been sent to France in anticipation of the heavy casualties of the Somme. However since the Hertfordshire Regiment only had one battalion on the battlefield it soon became over strength. This explains why men were attached or transferred to other regiments within the 39th Division such as the 11th, 12th and 13th Battalions of the Royal Sussex. Others were posted on the 30th October 1916 to the 1/8th Battalion Gloucestershire Regiment. Often when a man was wounded and recovered he too was posted to another regiment. A large number of Ware men who trained with the Herts were posted to the 6th Battalion Berkshire Regiment. This battalion comprised of mainly new recruits, probably the first to be called up when conscription was introduced under the Compulsory Service Act passed on the 25th January 1916. They were in action at Thiepval in late September, their success here enabling the Herts to capture St. Pierre Divion. Known casualties to Ware men transferred to these regiments are listed in *Appendix 4.*

The Battle of Ancre was the end of the battalion's involvement on the Somme front, and between the 15th and 19th of November they marched northwards to Orville Candas. Here they entrained to Esquelbecq followed by a march to Worm Houdt where they were billeted in huts. They were now back on the Ypres front.

Apart from Lieutenant Colonel Henry Page Croft no mention has been made so far of officers from Ware in the 1st Battalion, although the Ware Company was commanded by a local man, Captain Frank Hanbury Pawle from Widford. The reason is simple. When a man was promoted from within the ranks, he was posted to another Regiment where he would not be well known to the rank and file. One such man from the town was Captain Albert Hawkes MC. Albert was the son of William Hawkes of Star Street and joined the "Herts Terriers" in September 1914 going to France in November 1914. He is the same man who sang "Little Grey Home in the West" at Christmas 1914 and was well known throughout the Regiment for his magnificent voice, being called the "Herts Lark". He served with the Hertfordshire Regiment until the Battle of Ancre where he was an acting Company Sergeant Major. He then took a commission and was posted to the Bedfordshire Regiment with whom he won a Military Cross at Cambrai and was severely wounded early in 1918. Another "ranker" to take a commission was Captain F Whitby of London Road. Like Albert

Hawkes he enlisted in September 1914 and went to France in the following November. He had reached the rank of Sergeant by October 1916 when he returned for cadet training at Newmarket and returned to France in May 1917 with the 19th Battalion London Regiment (St Pancras Rifles). Leslie Delozey also took a commission in the 6th Battalion North Staffordshire Regiment on the 29th May 1918. Other officers from the town serving in Regiments other than the Hertfordshires and who were killed in the war are to be found in *Appendix 1*.

On the 29th November the battalion was on the move again by train and road to Popperinghe. From there they went on to Ypres to support dugouts beside the canal north of the town on temporary attachment to the 114th Brigade, before rejoining the 118th on the 15th December. The 118th were in the "Hill Top" sector (near St Jean) of the Ypres Canal and based in the left canal bank dugouts.

Christmas 1916 was spent in billets in the canal dugouts where they remained until the 3rd January 1917. This year "Our Boys" received presents from "The 1st Herts Cigarettes Fund" as well as parcels from "Ware Boys at the Front Fund". The first named fund was registered as a charity on the 25th October 1916 and run by Lady Longmore, the wife of Colonel Sir Charles Longmore, commander of the Reserve Battalion. The funds were raised by public subscription. On the 6th November 1916 Lady Longmore purchased the following from WH Frogley, Cigar and Cigarette Dealer, of 27 Fore Street, Hertford:

20,000 Woodbines	£ 9–0s–0d.
17,500 Goldflake	£12–5s–0d.
100 Goldflake to L/Cpl Easter of the 2/5th Gloucesters	3s–7d.
500 Abdulla to Colonel Page	£1–1s–3d.
1,000 Woodbines to the CO 8th Gloucester Regiment for the men of the 1st Herts	9s–0d.
50 Goldflake and postage to L/Cpl Ruskin in hospital at Warrington	1s–10d.
Total cost	£23–0s–8d.

There was also a "Herts Comfort Fund" which raised money through flag days to buy wool and other materials. In 1916 they purchased some 300lbs of wool which one presumes was knitted into balaclavas, scarves and socks by women's organisations and schools as was the case in the Second World War.

Chapter 8
1917

Throughout January and most of February 1917 the battalion were in and out of the front line trenches in the Wieltje sector returning to their support dugouts by the Ypres Canal. It was at Wieltje that Corporal J Wall, the son of Mr and Mrs Wall of Priory Street, was wounded when the battalion came under a heavy bombardment as it was being relieved on the 12th January. He was evacuated from France to a Red Cross hospital in Gloucester.

In the middle of February a party of three officers and sixty-four men from the battalion raided the German trenches at "Cambrai Trench" near Wieltje. The objective was to capture prisoners for identification purposes and the raid was a success with the Hertfordshire lads capturing two prisoners without incurring any casualties themselves. A few nights later the Germans raided the Hertfordshires who were holding the trenches in the "Observatory Ridge Sector". The raid was repulsed successfully.

The 17th February saw the "Herts Guards" marching away from the lines to "Y" Camp outside Poperinghe. Here they would have rested, used the mobile baths and been issued with clean clothing as well as enjoying the recreational facilities provided by the YMCA and other similar organisations. Ten days later they marched through Poperinghe to St Lawrence Camp and a few days later were marching again to their Divisional Reserve HQ at Kruistract.

However they soon returned to their old positions at the Front in the Observatory Sector at Wieltje where they remained for the whole of March. During this tour Private Fred Hart MM of 12 Priory Street was wounded. At the end of the month the battalion changed their location, marching to the infantry barracks at Ypres before spending a couple of days in the lines at Hooge. They were relieved on the 3rd April and moved by train back to St Lawrence Camp and on to billets at Houtkerque. For the next two weeks they were engaged in constructing a new railway, one of many narrow gauge lines laid out by the Royal Engineers leading up to the Front from the camps in the rear.

At the end of April the 1st Battalion were back in the front lines at Wieltje where they stayed for a month before marching back to Worm Hoult. The whole of June it appears that they marched from camp to camp gradually making their way back to the Hilltop Sector at Ypres on the 1st July. It was here that Private George Clark of Ware was killed on the 3rd July. They remained in this sector until the 17th July when they marched from their support trenches back to Poperinghe and on to Houle near St Omer.

Chapter 9
THE THIRD BATTLE OF YPRES – JULY 1917

At St Omer their division, the 39th, received special training for two weeks in preparation for a forthcoming offensive. The aim of the planned Allied offensive was to break out of the Ypres Salient by pushing eastwards across Flanders and possibly linking up with a British sea-borne invasion along the Belgian coast. To this end British troops were in "closed camps" along the French coast practising landings from barges and scaling sea walls. The offensive became known as the Third Battle of Ypres. During the training it was emphasised that a main feature of the attack was to be an artillery barrage of immense weight which would enable the infantry to move forward without the inconvenience of enemy small arms fire. Four tanks were to be allotted to deal with any unforeseen circumstances.

The first phase of the Third Battle of Ypres was to remove the Germans from their vantage point on the Messines Ridge. This was achieved in June 1917. The

A tenting party from the Herts Guards somewhere in France. They were in good spirits – note the wag in the second row with his mallet raised. The photograph was taken before April 1916 when Bill Presland (back row, third from the right) and Ernest Page (fourth from the right) were discharged at the end of their Territorial service: they both then joined the Royal Horse Artillery.

second phase of the offensive was to recapture the central and northern sectors of the salient and in particular the Passchendaele Ridge and this was to last from the 31st July until the 6th November.

What the planners overlooked was the effect that rain combined with heavy shell fire would have on the ground. The attack, made over a front of some fifteen miles, with the main assault in the centre was being undertaken by the British 5th Army. For several weeks before the attack the German positions had been subjected to a fierce and prolonged artillery bombardment, which in theory would destroy the German forward lines built in the dry on the higher ground and breach the masses of barbed wire entanglements in front of these bunkers. Constant rain through the summer had turned the Flanders clay into a quagmire and all the bombardment by our heavy guns achieved was to make things worse by destroying field drains and stream banks and making it impossible for tanks to support the advance. The Germans in the meantime sat out the bombardment in their dry underground bunkers.

The Advance on St Julian, Pilkem Ridge

Immediately the 1st Battalion of the Hertfordshire Regiment finished their training they moved back to the Front at Ypres on the 29th July to take part in the second phase. Their division was to attack the centre in front of the village of St Julien and had been allotted three objectives known as the Blue, Black and Green lines – an advance of some 3000 yards. The "Green Line" was the Langemarck–Zonnebeke Road. During the night of Monday 30th July the Herts Battalion was in its assembly positions in X lines in the Hill Top Sector having marched from Veamertinge under shell fire which caused a few casualties. Their actual advance is described without any emotion in the battalion diary upon which the next paragraph is based.

Zero hour for the attack was set at 3.50 am on the 31st July just as dawn was breaking and the battalion formed up in four lines. It was raining of course. The initial advance behind a "creeping barrage" was undertaken by the regiments in the 116th and 117th Brigades which quickly captured the Blue and Black lines – the first two enemy defences. The Hertfordshires moved forward from their assembly position at 5.00 am and soon reached the Front at the Black line. Here they paused for a while before they passed through the troops of the 116th Brigade comprising the 11th, 12th and 13th Battalions Royal Sussex and advanced to the east of the River Steenbeck. Until now the casualties had been very light but as the advance continued from the Steenbeck stream towards their objective of the Langemarck or Green line, they sustained heavier casualties from sniper and machine-gun fire. However the battalion continued advancing. About half way to the objective some of No 3 Company, the men from Ware and Watford, under the command of Lieutenant Gallo came upon a German strong point which they gallantly charged and captured, killing most of the garrison and sending the remainder back as prisoners. On reaching the enemy wire it was found to be very thick and undamaged, except in one place. Second Lieutenant Marchington and a handful of men from No 3 Company got through the only gap and into the enemy trench killing many of the occupying Germans. The rest of the battalion being unable to get through the wire and suffering severe casualties from flanking machine-gun fire together with a strong German counter attack on their left flank were forced to fall back. The remainder of the battalion subsequently dug themselves in line with the 1st Cambridgeshires on the west bank of the Steenbeek.

This modest description from the battalion diary warrants expansion since the battalion suffered such severe casualties that by the end of the day every officer was killed or wounded and well over half of the other ranks were killed, wounded or missing. A letter in the *Mercury* of the 11th August from a soldier in the Herts Regiment describing the conditions said that "the 'big push' took place in rain across ploughed up ground and that with every step one sank deep down past ones knee". Other sources, particularly an unpublished book by Lieut Col B J Gripper, an officer in the battalion, give more detail. He tells us that the attack formation of the Herts when they advanced through the 116th Brigade was as follows:

The forward companies were No 1 on the right under Lieutenant Hardy and No 2 on the left under Captain S Lowery. The support companies were No 3 under Lieutenant Gallo on the right with No 4 under Captain Fisher on the left.

In front of the Hertfordshires was a wide band of uncut barbed wire but fortunately for them one of the four tanks managed to slide through the edge of the creeping barrage and flatten it at the same time driving the German garrison behind into their dugouts. This action allowed the Herts lads to press into St Julien, which was only lightly held, and capture it by 10 o'clock, taking many prisoners together with a battery of thirteen 5.9 inch howitzers and its large ammunition dump.

The 1st Battalion, with some difficulty, crossed the Steenbeek where two of its tanks became permanently bogged down. Thereafter things went from bad to worse. The much vaunted barrage which was to carry the Hertfordshires forward to the Green line did not materialise since it was impossible to move the guns forward due to the terrible ground conditions; in fact the ground was so bad that shells were taken to the guns by mule train since it was impossible to use the usual limbers. Ground could only be won by "section rushes" supported by the unit's own fire power. The 1st Battalion of the Cambridgeshire Regiment on the battalion's right managed to keep in touch and level with them but their left flank was exposed since the 4th/5th Black Watch Regiment advancing over more difficult ground had been seriously delayed.

The advance continued slowly but by 10.30 am it was clear that the Green line would not be captured. The casualties had been heavy including the Commanders of number 1 and 3 companies (Lieutenants Hardy and Gallo).

In spite of heavy machine gun fire the Herts continued their advance and the their gallantry did not go unnoticed. The Press Bureau sanctioned the publication in the *Daily Mail* of a description from the pen of Mr W Beech Thomas, a well known war correspondent, of the fighting in which the Herts men suffered such severe casualties. The highest sacrifice in the Third Battle of Ypres, wrote Mr Beech Thomas, was perhaps paid by the Hertfordshire Regiment who, with other Territorials as gallant as themselves, took St Julien and pushed forward deep into the enemy country beyond. Thomas took up the account after the fall of St Julien:

At or about 10 o'clock, after St Julien was captured and, indeed, the core of the battle won, the German shelling with 5.9inch howitzers grew hotter than many officers had ever seen, and it had various effects. In front of one little knot of men dodging shells under very cool and expert leadership there broke such an explosion that all believed a land mine had gone up. But in spite of it all, the shock and continuous bursting of this noisiest of all shells, the men felt quite safe and comfortable in their shell hole. As one of them said, when they got out of it after the earth had stopped shaking, they found that the land mine was in fact the captured German dump of shells which had been hit by the German artillery".

Losing men all the time, but never checked, these troops pushed on a good 1200 yards to the next line of trenches. One officer was wounded and set on fire by a fragment of shell which exploded some of the SOS lights in his pocket. He put out the fire by rolling over and over in the mud. The wound he disregarded and carried on as before, but without his signals and a good part of his clothing. Such was the conduct of the regiment reduced in numbers, but not in spirit. The men reached the approaches to a trench defended by 400 yards of uncut wire six yards deep and running along a contour swept by machine-guns from the left, front and flank. Some made their way round it, some hacked at the wire and forced a way over it. They took the trench, with a good number of prisoners, and began to consolidate.

While his forward troops were attacking the trench described above, the battalion commander, Lieut Col Frank Page, was trying to organise reinforcements near Steenbeek when he was killed by a shell. The following description of the CO's death was a letter published in the *Mercury* from Signaller Walter Page writing home from Bagthorpe Military Hospital in Nottingham:

I have just arrived back from the severest fighting our regiment has experienced. We have suffered very heavy casualties but we won the day. I was just behind

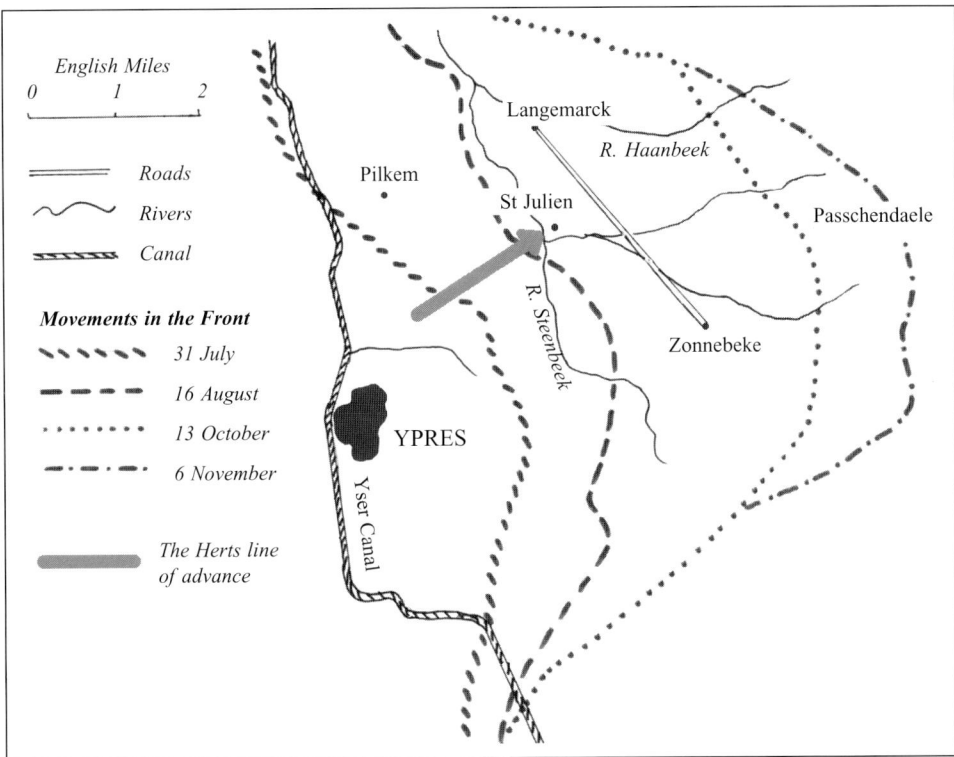

English Miles
0   1   2

════════ Roads
〜〜〜 Rivers
▨▨▨▨ Canal

Movements in the Front
＼＼＼＼ 31 July
▬ ▬ ▬ ▬ 16 August
• • • • • • 13 October
▬·▬·▬· 6 November

━━━━ The Herts line
of advance

Langemarck

R. Haanbeek

Pilkem

St Julien

Passchendaele

R. Steenbeek

Zonnebeke

YPRES

Yser Canal

The Third Battle of Ypres and Passchendaele – July to November 1917

our famous Colonel when he got killed, and also the Adjutant (Captain Milne) and Captain (Captain Lowery). I am afraid we have had a good number taken prisoners, for the Hun counter-attacked and cut some of our men off. The Regiment fought well. I am shot badly through both thighs, but I am going on satisfactory. The remnant of the Regiment is now back at rest.

Walter Page obviously understated the details of Lt Col Page's death. Since he has no known grave and is commemorated on the Menim Gate at Ypres, he was probably blown to pieces.

Walter Page described in the *Hertfordshire Countryside* the awful conditions the wounded suffered. After he was shot he crawled back to the village of St Julien where two German prisoners were ordered to carry him to the dressing station. Here his trousers were cut off and field bandages applied to his wounds.

It seemed ironical that a few minutes earlier I was shooting at Germans and now I had my arms around two of them as they carried me down the line. I lay in a dugout for two days, having jabs of morphine as I was in great pain. My field dressings were soaked in blood and mud. It rained for three whole days. The stretcher bearers carried me knee deep in mud to the canal bank dressing station. After my wounds were dressed I was transported to Boulogne and from there I boarded the hospital ship *St Andrew* to Dover and on to Bagthorpe.

Here he spent nine months recovering and then volunteered to go back to France which he did in August 1918.

To return to Mr Thomas's account of the action published in the *Daily Mail* he described what happened after the Herts battalion captured the trench:

Somewhere about this time the last of the officers in the Hertfordshire Regiment fell and a sergeant, himself severely wounded took command (this was RSM Tite from Tring). In front of this occupied trench was a shallow ditch manned by a considerable garrison of the enemy, who threw up their hands and came forward to give themselves up, when the sound of machine-gun fire was heard away in the rear of the Territorials. Both Germans and British saw more or less what happened. The Hertfordshires and Cambridgeshires had advanced almost alone. A wide space on one flank was occupied by just four men, and the ground now far in the rear was still occupied by the enemy. Very much the same thing was developing on the other flank. The surrendered prisoners suddenly appreciating the position took up arms again, and even prisoners in their midst attempted to fight. The Territorials were more than surrounded, if one may say so, for they were also mixed up with the enemy, but they fought on. They shot scores of the enemy in the Front, especially among those who had taken up arms after surrendering, and they dealt with a full dress model counter-attack, carried through to the letter, according to the new German formula, in waves of some 150 yards apart. They even had time to see some German field guns move forward under the lee of a hill to their right front.

At last in the afternoon, when it was found that so few men from the troops on the flank had got through and the machine-guns continued to fire from their rear, they decided to fight their way back, and they fought back quite undefeated, though every officer was gone and most of the NCOs. Among the men still with them was the padre, the Revd E Popham MC, a chaplain of many fights, who cheered them on and at the end, being the last man to cross a little stream, carried, and when he could no longer carry, dragged a wounded man to safer quarters a mile or more in the rear. But this was later. (For his gallantry Popham was awarded a bar to the MC he already held).

As they struggled back towards St Julien, a group of Germans who had thrust through from their flank held up their hands in surrender and called out for mercy. It happened that at the same time the German counter-attack from the opposite flank had made some progress, and their men and these men, seeing their fellows surrendering ruthlessly turned their machine-guns on their own kin. No more ghastly plight could be imagined. If they surrendered, their own men shot them. If they took up arms, they proved themselves traitors as well as enemies and were shot down by us.

Nor was that all. The German artillery about this hour received orders to barrage the whole field, and 5.9 inch shells, mixed with some high velocity shells, fell indiscriminately on prisoners, on German attackers, and on our troops fighting homewards. In the worst of the confusion our men kept a clear head, and at last, thanks in great measure to the skilful assistance of their friends in reserve, fighting all the way, but now almost without ammunition, they came through. Some of these supporting companies occupied a small hillock and set up in position as many as thirteen machine and Lewis guns. These raked the Germans both on the left and right front and did great havoc. Though our losses were perhaps heavier here than at any part of the fifteen mile battle front, the enemy's losses were probably on yet a greater scale.

I write especially of a regiment known to me personally better than any regiment in the Army, and one weighs one's words with special care in writing of friends. The fight was one of the stoutest fights of the war, worthy of the Guards at the First Battle of Ypres. The men were "Hertfordshire Guards" indeed, and their homes should ring with their story of sacrifice and valour".

Yet another account of the atrocious conditions encountered came from No 3 Company's Quartermaster, Joseph Ketterer from Ware. Normally the evening's rations were brought from the transport lines some five or six miles from the rear on limbers. However at the end of July the mud was so bad that they had to use panniers on pack mules and even then the Transport Officer refused to take the mules beyond the original German front lines since they were in danger of being bogged down. The rations were unloaded and the "Quarters" set out to find the battalion and organise carrying parties only to be told that it had been decimated. The rations were given to any passing troops apart from one two-gallon container of rum which the Quartermasters kept for themselves for the long trek back through the mud and rain to the transport lines – and also to give them courage to tell the few remaining troops that the battalion had been wiped out.

The following morning the Herts Regiment gained another distinction. The Brigade Commander ordered Padre Popham to take charge of the remnants of the 1st Herts and for a short time it may be said that a chaplain was in command of a battalion which is probably unique. In the evening Major E C M Phillips came forward and took command.

What price did the battalion pay in this action? They lost their Commanding Officer and six other officers killed, six more were wounded and four taken prisoner.

Casualties among the other ranks numbered 459 – of these 136 were killed or missing and 323 wounded. As a fighting unit the Herts had temporarily ceased to exist.

The known casualties from Ware serving with the 1st Battalion Hertfordshire Regiment at St Julien were:

Killed or died of wounds:
— Sergeant Hiram Hammond of Kibes Lane;
— Private Harry Parnell of Cross Street;
— Sergeant George Reynolds MM of London Road;
— Private Claud Sweeney MM of London Road;
— Private Charles Salmons of New Hill Cottages, Near Ware;
— Private Herbert G Clibbon of 4, Redan Road, Musley Hill (enlisted in the Herts Regt., transferred to the Royal Sussex Regiment, killed at St Julien);
— Corporal James A Skinner of Holywell Hill, St Albans, (he was born in Ware but his family moved to St Albans during the war).

Prisoners of War:
— Private Sydney Presland of Baldock Street, held at Darmstadt;
— Private Arthur Saunders of Star Street, held at Limberg.

Wounded:
— Lance Corporal Richard Cockman MM;
— Signaller Walter E Page of 40 Crib Street, wounded in both thighs;
— Private Ernest Martin of 156 Musley Hill;
— Private Charles Johnson;
— Private F Cadmore;
— Private T Levy wounded in the right arm on August 1st (he was transferred to hospital at Newport in Wales);
— Private Thomas Ives of 9, Chapel Yard, Amwell End;
— Sergeant Alfred Ensby MM;
— Sergeant William Gaines MM of 13 Vicarage Road;
— Private Samuel Campkin of Bury Field Terrace (for the fourth time);
— Private E B Hitch of Kibes Lane;
— Corporal Richard Page MM of Bowling Road;
— Private Alfred Page of 32 Crib Street;
— Private George Skeggs of Baldock Street;
— Lance Corporal H Ablett;
— Private Thomas Skipp of 61 New Road attached to the Royal Sussex Regt.

Through their gallantry men of the 1st Battalion were awarded twelve Military Medals and five Sergeants received the Distinguished Conduct Medal. Four Ware men, Lance Sergeants W Gaines and A Ensby together with Lance Corporal R Cockman and Private E J Marshall received the Military Medal. The officer who led the men from No.3 Company through the gap in the wire and was wounded, Second Lieutenant E W Marchington, received the Military Cross.

Not surprisingly there are no entries in the battalion's diary for the 1st August 1917. The next day Major Philips, Captain Whitehead and Second Lieutenant EM Paul went up to the line to take charge of the 130 other ranks who remained from the fight of the 31st July. This group remained over night in positions called the Tower Post and Irish Farm. The survivors moved forward in support of the 116th Brigade staying in the old German front line system until the 5th August. Conditions must have been really bad to warrant an entry in the battalion diary which said "the trenches being in a terrible condition owing to almost continuous rain since the evening of the 31st July".

The battalion pulled out of the line on the 5th August moving to a bivouac camp at Reigersbury Chateau – hardly the ideal summer for camping! – before en-training at Vlamertinghe (just outside Ypres) for Caestre and then by bus to a camp near Thiehshouk. Here they were addressed and inspected by the Top Brass and no doubt being told what "good boys" they had been – and I make no apologises for being cynical. During their stay here several drafts of men, totalling 167 in all, were posted to the battalion before they made their way back to the Front by bus on the 14th August to their Divisional Reserve Camp near Ridge Wood. Spells in the front lines in the Klein Zillebeke lines were undertaken before they marched back to Ascot Camp at Westoutre some ten miles south west of Ypres. At Ascot Camp another 282 men were posted to the battalion which re-equipped.

On the 19th September fourteen officers together with 556 other ranks marched in fighting order for "forthcoming operations" to Zwarteleen, the remainder of the battalion going to the Divisional Reserve Camp. They were going into action to the south of the infamous Ypres – Menim Road in the neighbourhood of Hollebeke. The attack was launched the next day with the Herts Regiment held in reserve in the support lines. They moved into the newly-won front lines in the Shrewsbury Forest area for a day on the 23rd before retiring to Corunna Camp near Wesoutre on the 27th September. During this ten-day spell, the battalion suffered over two hundred casualties through heavy hostile shelling in the front line. Two Ware men were killed in this short spell – Private Thomas Saunders of Willow Wharf who died on the 21st September in the support lines at Bugler Wood, and Private Ernest Adams of 53 High Oak Road who was killed holding the front line on the 23th September. Other Ware men were wounded, among them Private F Gayler of Star Street (wounded for the second time), and Lance Sergeant W Greenhill. For the first time the battal-ion records the fact that men suffered from shell shock.

At Corunna Camp the recipients of awards won at St Julien were presented with their medal ribbons. They soon moved back to Ypres and most of October was spent working on railway lines between Westhoek and Zonnebeke. The battalion gave a concert in the YMCA hut before returning to the lines in Tower Hamlets sector, south of the Menim Road. Normal trench routine took place for a month in which they were attacked by gas – trench foot was a problem too. It was probably here that 2655 Private Charles E Smith of Ware was wounded.

In September 1917 the 1st Reserve Battalion back at home was absorbed with the 5th Reserve Battalion of the Bedfordshire Regiment. This combined Battalion had "Beds" and "Herts" wings and has been mistakenly known as "the Beds and Herts Regiment" which was not in fact formed until July 1919. Men from Ware such as John Gray DCM, Fred Hart MM, Solomon Trundle and Ernest Martin, who were wounded at the Battle of Ancre, must have been posted to the 5th Reserve Battalion when they had recovered from their injuries back in England. This explains why they were posted to various battalions of the Bedfordshire Regiment on their return to France. Others such as William Hart were to go to more "exotic" places. Hart joined 4/4th Battalion of the King's African Rifles which was formed at the Eastern Command School of Instruction based at Hertford in September 1917. He sailed for East Africa from Devonport on the 11th October 1917 on the troopship *Port Melbourne* via Freetown, Cape Town and Durban. In Africa he learnt Swahili and caught malaria. He left East Africa for "demob" towards the end of February 1919.

Back in France, Corporal Alfred E Baker, possibly from Trinity Road, was awarded the DCM in October but unfortunately his citation no longer exists. Towards the end of November the battalion had a three day break at Eecke Aroa cleaning up, before returning to Ypres where they were out of the lines on fatigue duties and training. The battalion diary records that the men spent a happy Christmas Day as a result of the various gifts and comforts provided for them. Their Christmas respite over, the battalion moved back into the lines on the 31st December to the Hill Top Farm area near St Jean. Conditions were hard since part of their time was spent under canvas.

During 1917 several men who had enlisted in the Herts Regiment were transferred to other units. For example a batch of men who had served in the 1st Battalion throughout 1915–1916 were transferred to the Northumberland Fusiliers. A photograph published in the *Midweek Mercury* on the 4th November 1975 shows a group of thirty-two men said to be from Ware and Hertford in their new Regiment.

Chapter 10
1918 AND THE RETURN TO THE SOMME

On the 21st January the 39th Division including the 1st Herts Battalion pulled out of the Ypres battle fields. They entrained at Proven, some ten miles to the west of Ypres, moving south by train and foot to Peronne via Mericourt L'Abbe and Bray-sur-Somme to a tented camp at Haut Allaines. They now formed part of the British 5th Army and were back at the Somme. On the 8th February the Herts Regiment was transferred to the 116th Infantry Brigade and moved to Church Camp at Heudicourt. Their new companions in the Brigade were the 11th and 13th Battalions Royal Sussex Regiment, both of which battalions contained Ware men.

They were to move into the lines the next day in the Gouzeaucourt sector where they remained until mid March. This was a relatively quiet period at the Front apart from raids made by both sides to obtain the identity of troops facing them. It was during such a raid by the Germans on the 6th March 1918 that Sergeant William Gaines won a bar to the Military Medal he gained at St Julien. A report in the *Mercury* said:

Sergeant W Gaines 256176 of the Herts Regiment was wounded at St Julien on July 31st last and was subsequently awarded the MM for his coolness and bravery in that terrible battle in which the Herts men suffered so heavily. He has now gained further distinction in the form of a bar to his Military Medal. The circumstances are thus recorded: "For conspicuous gallantry and devotion to duty in the Gauche Wood sector (about one mile south of Gouzeaucourt) March 6th 1918. After a very heavy artillery and trench mortar bombardment Sergeant Gaines' company was raided by the enemy who succeeded in taking Private Kiddell prisoner. This man was wounded, dragged through the wire and finally abandoned by the enemy in a shell hole in "no man's land".

Sergeant Gaines with great gallantry went out and in spite of heavy shelling and machine gun fire dragged Private Kiddell as far as our wire. He then, with the assistance of another man, brought Private Kiddell into our trench.

Sergeant Gaines was the son of Mr and Mrs Gaines of 13 Vicarage Road, Ware. Private John Gray DCM was killed in action on the same day as Sergeant Gaines won the bar to his Military Medal.

The German Spring Offensive of March 1918

The Hertfordshire Regiment and their comrades in the 116th Brigade remained with the 39th Division which now formed part of the VII Army Corps. When the German Spring Offensive on the Somme broke on the 21st March their Division was in reserve, the front line being held by the 9th, 16th and 21st Divisions between Gouzeaucourt and Lempire.

The German's assault on the VII Corps started in the early hours of the morning with the main thrust being made against the 16th Division on the right flank. At 1.45 pm the 116th Brigade in its assembly position at Gurlu Wood was placed under the orders of the 16th Division. The Hertfordshires moved forward in the afternoon towards the retreating 16th Division. When they reached Villers Faucon they heard of the magnitude of the enemy success when a Brigade Commander of the 16th Division told of the virtual destruction of his brigade. The Hertfordshires took up their positions around Villers Faucon near St Emile. On the 22nd March the Hertfordshires were heavily engaged in the recapture of St Emile and later in the day they received orders to retire to new lines near Tincourt (east of Peronne). During the retreat there was much confused fighting and they were heavily shelled suffering many casualties.

The "Herts Guards" were on the march again before dawn on the 23rd and put

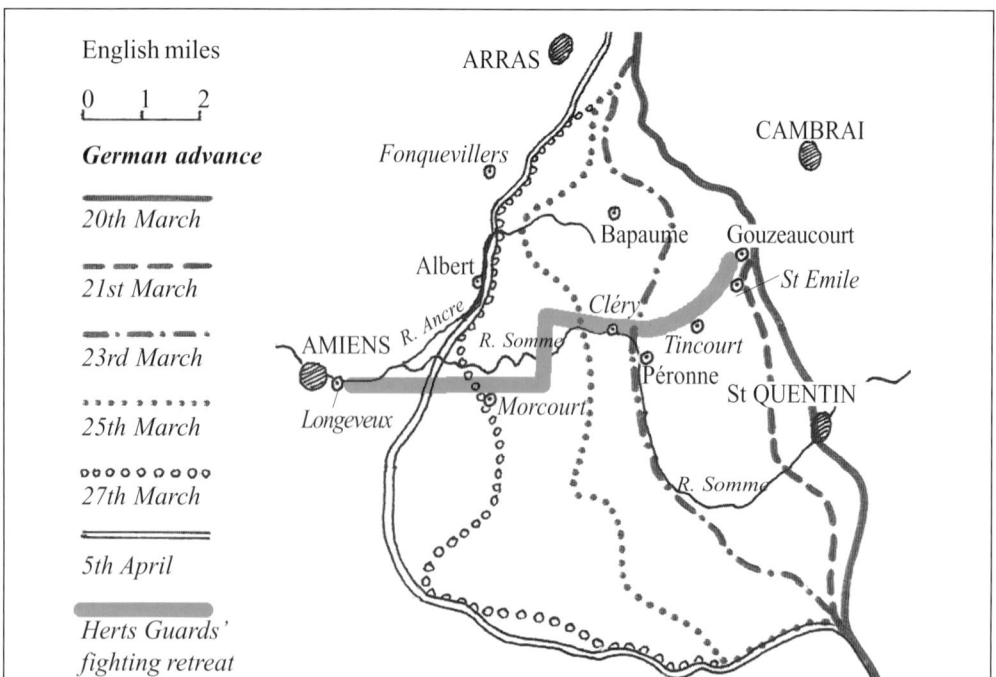

The advances made by German forces in their Spring Offensive of 1918

up stubborn resistance in the retreat towards the village of Cléry where they dug in and defended a line of trenches behind the village running down the River Somme. By the end of the night the only officers left with the 1st Battalion were their Commanding Officer, Lieut-Col Phillips, Major Clerk and six others.

After an intense bombardment on the morning of the 24th the Germans attacked the "Herts Guards" lines in large numbers forcing them to retire westwards to Fevillers and on to Maricourt where they spent the night. During the retreat part of the battalion was cut off and surrounded and taken prisoner including the Commanding Officer and four men from Ware. Major A G Clerk assumed command of the battalion. The retreat continued. On the 25th they left Maricourt and over the next six days fought a rearguard action via Insaunne, crossing the Somme at Cappy, then on to Ghuignolles, Proyart and Bois de Hangard and back to Longeveux, a small village on the outskirts of Amiens. They arrived here on the 31st March with the remnants of the battalion being commanded by the only surviving officer.

At midnight on the 25th March, after ten days of continual fighting, the Herts Battalion travelled by bus to Guigemicourt to regather and count their loses. Four officers and twenty five other ranks had been killed and two more officers and ten other ranks were wounded and missing. The number of wounded was not recorded but must have been considerable.

Sergeant George Adams was awarded the Military Medal for his gallantry during the retreat. The recommendation for the award read:

> for conspicuous gallantry and devotion to duty during the counter attack at Aubercourt on the 27th March when he led his men with the greatest of bravery under exceptionally trying conditions. This NCO did excellent work throughout the operations from the 22nd to the 31st March 1918, his coolness and courage throughout was the greatest assistance and he was chiefly instrumental in keeping his men together during the retreat.

It was some time before the official casualty lists filtered through but when they did they were truly horrendous. Ware grieved with the rest of the county. Ware men posted as casualties in the lists were:

Killed or died of wounds:
— 266230 Sergeant A H Wilbourn of High Oak Road killed 30th March;
— 265147 Acting Sergeant-Major Edward Clark of Ware killed 24th March;
— 266008 Sergeant James Walsingham of 6 Amwell End taken prisoner and died of his wounds on the 28th June 1918;
— 265773 Private Robert Williams of Ware died of his wounds on the 29th April.

Prisoners of war:
— 265146 Sergeant Frederick Crook, 32 Gladstone Road;

— 265650 L/Cpl Samuel Campkin, 4 Buryfield Road – he had been wounded at Festubert in 1915 and gassed later in that year, wounded in the Battle of Ancre in 1916 and again at St Julien in 1917;

— 4380 Private Ernest Hatherhill, 29 Garland Road;

— 266007 Private F Nash.

Wounded:

— 265931 Sergeant George Adams MM (for the third time);

— 265630 L/Sergeant Alfred Baker DCM;

— 266648 Private T Cakebread;

— 267387 Private F J Chalkley;

— 265176 Sergeant William Gaines MM and bar;

— 266340 Private William Maling;

— 265277 Corporal Harry Wallace Page;

— 266275 Private J Wallace of Baldock Street;

— 265845 Private Harry Winter MM;

— 1706 Drummer William T Hills of 154 Musley Hill, wounded on 30th March with three bullet wounds in his right foot.

From Guignemicourt the remainder of the "Herts Guards" travelled to billets at St Marin-au-Laert, near St Omer, and then back to the Ypres battle front. Their brigade had suffered such terrible losses that orders were received for the 1st Herts Battalion to form half a composite battalion with the remnants of the 11th Battalion the Royal Sussex Regiment. Their respite was short lived. During the night of the 10th/11th April they were on the move again going by train to Vlamertinghe. Here the battalion reorganised and "D Company" of the new battalion was formed out of the original Nos 3 and 4 Companies with Captain A G Grinling as their company commander. The next day they moved to Otago Camp near Hooge before going into the Voormezeele sector to strengthen the support lines.

Chapter 11
THE THIRD BATTLE OF LYS – APRIL 1918

The Germans launched their spring offensive south of Ypres on the 8th April 1918. Voormezeele was at the northern end of the Front some five miles south of the town of Ypres – compared with the areas further south it had been relatively quiet. However on the 24th April the Germans attacked Wytschaete (known as "Whitesheets" to the Tommies). The next day the remnants of the Herts and Royal Sussex were subjected to a very heavy bombardment of shrapnel and gas shells and their line was heavily attacked at 6 o'clock in the morning but the German attack was repulsed.

It was here that Acting Sergeant Thomas Martin of London Road and Lance Corporal Richard Cockman MM were killed on the 26th April and Private Robert Williams received wounds from which he died on the 29th April. All three were from Ware. The battalion remained under heavy shell fire until the 28th when they were relieved and marched back to Devonshire Camp where they rested being exhausted after fourteen days in the trenches.

After reorganising and further consolidation of their companies they moved back from the Front and gradually worked their way to Candas (a few miles south west of Doullens) by the 9th May. They were back on the Somme. Here they were transferred to the 37th Division and were conveyed to Orville where the battalion spent two nights in the open.

On the 11th May the 1st Herts Battalion enbussed at Orville at 5 pm for Souastra marching from there to a line of old British trenches to the east of Fonquevillers, north of the town of Albert. As they marched through the village of Fonquevillers they were subjected to a very heavy gas shell bombardment. The Commanding Officer, Lieut Col R Wilkinson DSO and the remainder of the officers with the exception of Captain N P Gold were evacuated to hospital during the night. All the NCOs and men except for seven were also taken to hospital. The following morning Captain Gold and the seven remaining men made their way back to the battalion's transport section but later in the day Captain Gold and five of the seven were taken to a casualty clearing station. Out of some 600 front line troops only two came through the gas attack unscathed. The 1st Battalion Hertfordshire Regiment was effectively wiped out and was no longer a fighting unit.

How many men from Ware were wounded or suffered from the effects of gas at Voormezeele and Fonquevillers is uncertain but the following names appear in the extensive casualty lists published in June and July 1918:

265099 Private William T Hills of Crib Street;

265211 Private Charles Johnson;

265598 Corporal Ernest Andrews;

266244 Private Arthur Brett;

265728 Private Harry Cockman of Kibes Lane;

265265 Private Sidney A Ditton;

265104 Sergeant Harry Jackson;

265063 CSM Northrope.

The battalion's transport and QM stores were unaffected by the gas attack and moved on the 15th May to billets at Louvencourt on the main road from Albert to Doullens. Here they were joined by a draft from England of Captain S W Moore and 81 other ranks. On the 22nd May the remnants of the "Herts Guards" fighting men absorbed 30 officers and 650 other ranks from the 6th (Service) Battalion Bedfordshire Regiment but excluding their transport and training staff – the 6th Bedfordshires was then disbanded after the transfer of its fighting men into the Hertfordshires. Major R C Cartew MC from the Essex Regiment assumed command.

The next day the battalion marched to a new camp on the outskirts of the village of Vauchelles to the south west of Doullens. For a week they were in strict training – no doubt the 1st Battalion's training staff were bringing their new comrades from the Bedfordshires up to the standards expected of the "Herts Guards". The 1st Battalion Hertfordshire Regiment now formed part of the 112th Brigade, the 6th Bedfordshire's original brigade. During June the battalion trained and gradually made their way by a series of route marches and bus to Souastre. By the 25th of June they were in the reserve trenches at Fonquevillers – the same village where they were so badly gassed some six weeks previously. July 1918 was spent in the lines at Pigeon Wood with rest breaks in camp at Souastre.

Back on the home front another fete in aid of "The Ware Boys at the Front Fund" was held at Presdales on August Bank holiday. Over £200 was raised, £80 of which was taken at the gate which indicates that a considerable number of the town's people attended. The committee decided to donate £50 to "The Prisoners of War Help Committee (Herts Branch)" for the benefit of Ware men from the Herts and Beds regiments who were prisoners. The committee felt that this Fund needed liberal support, as the men depended mainly on parcels from the Fund for their sustenance. Stories of the hardships endured by the POWs were related by Ernest Page of Gladstone Road (he was a time served "Terrier" with the Herts Guards who had rejoined the forces with the Royal Horse Artillery and the Northumberland Fusiliers with whom he was taken prisoner). If the prisoners passed a mangold field while marching from camp to camp his comrades reckoned that if anyone could break ranks and pinch a few it was he. Ernest would secrete the mangolds in his large pockets – dare one ask if they were poacher's pockets? However Ernest was finally caught and sentenced to three days solitary confinement, his mates reckoning that as he was to have peace and quiet for three days with nothing to do he might as well repair their clothes. The joke was on them since Ernest was confined in an unlit room. After the war he returned to work in the maltings opposite Gladstone Road.

Around this time another fund was set up in the town, when Mr F T Barker of Baldock Street was appointed the secretary of the Ware fund to help blind soldiers.

Certificate.

BUTTONHOLE BADGE.

1st Hertfordshire Regiment, British Expeditionary Force, 1914 to 1919.

No. *586*

has been issued to *No. 268332   Sgt. W. C. Hart.*

in recognition of his services overseas with the Regiment.

LIEUT.-COL.
Secretary T.F. Association, Herts.

HERTFORD,
26 :— 7 :— 1919.

SIMSON & CO., LTD.

Sergeant William Hart's Buttonhole Badge certificate

Chapter 12
THE ADVANCE TO VICTORY

On the 8th August the Allies started their Somme offensive. Initially the Hertford-shire Regiment and their comrades in the 112th Brigade were held in reserve in the Pigeon Wood area. Private Walter Page returned to the 1st Battalion after some nine months recovering from his wounds received at St Julien. He commented that all the old faces he knew were missing. One can only assume that the few men – such as Drummer Edmund Parker of Coronation Road – who spent the whole of the war in France and returned home unscathed were either in the battalion's training, stores or transport sections. Page was severely wounded in the left arm on the 18th August – the fourth time he been wounded during the war – and was still in hospital at Trouville when the Armistice was signed.

As part of the Allied offensive the 112th Brigade led the attack against a rail-way cutting in front of Achiet-le-Grand, which was taken on the 23rd August, and broke through the Hindenburg Line. Two other Ware men were wounded during this period – Sergeant Joseph Brinklow of Crib Street and Private George Skeggs from Baldock Street.

Most of September was spent in the lines attacking the enemy front before moving back to billets and hutments at Warlincourt. Here the battalion reorganised once again before moving back to a camp on the Fremicourt–Lebeucqueire Road. They stayed a couple of days and then moved into the trenches at "Dead Man's Corner" near Gouzeaucourt where they had started their long retreat under the weight of the German Spring Offensive the previous March.

The battle to recapture Cambrai started on the 8th October with the 37th Divi-sion among the forward Divisions pushing eastwards to the south of Cambrai. The Herts Regiment pressed forward crossing the Selle River and advanced towards Caudry and the village of Gaissignes. On the 27th October they moved out of the line to Beaurain where they were billeted in a large farm before returning to the Front at Bernier Farm on the 3rd November. The battalion launched its final attack against the Germans on the following day when they successfully captured the vil-lages of Chissignes and Louvinges and pushed forward to the village of Lolimetz. During the advance Privates Harry Winter MM and Joshua Page of 40 Crib Street (the brother of Walter Page) were wounded – the last known casualties of the "Herts Guards" from Ware. On the 4th November they came out of the lines for the last time and withdrew to Ghissignes.

Chapter 13
THE ARMISTICE AND POST WAR

The 11th November 1918, Armistice Day, found the 1st Battalion Hertfordshire Regiment on the march, making their way to Bry where they remained until mid-December. It was from here that a colour party left for Hertford to collect the battalion's colours which had been laid up in St Andrews Church since August 1914.

The battalion left Bry on the 14th December marching via Bellignes, La Longueville, Maubeuge, Trazegnies to Ransart some four miles north-east of Charleroi. This was to be "home" until the end of February 1919. Here gradual demobilisation took place and time was spent taking part in sports and educational classes.

Some men had returned home before the general demobilisation, possibly after the gas attacks on the regiment earlier in the year. One such man was Drummer James Cockman of 67 Watton Road. He went to France with the 1st Battalion in 1914 and was married in Ware a week before Christmas 1918 – a far happier one than the previous four all spent in France. In other cases their pre-war employers successfully pressed for their early release. In addition to their discharge papers each man was given a regimental buttonhole badge and a payment on account, pending final settlement of his pay.

With the war over the committee for "The Ware Boys at the Front Fund" had surplus funds and on Wednesday the 29th January 1919 gave a dinner at the Drill Hall in Amwell End to commemorate the cessation of hostilities. Invitations were sent to all men whose homes were in or near the town and something like 200 responded. Some 171 men sat down to a meal prepared by Mr George Edwards comprising soup, roast beef, roast and boiled mutton, roast pork, baked and boiled potatoes, brussel sprouts and parsnips, followed by ginger and fruit pudding with beer, lemonade, coffee and cigarettes *ad lib*. Music throughout the evening was played by Mr R Langton Bones' orchestra. Patriotic speeches were made and the troops were entertained by conjuring tricks, humorous ditties, clog dancing and songs. A list of attendees is given in *Appendix 5*.

Around this time the returning servicemen set up the "Ware and District Ex-servicemen's Association", the forerunner of the British Legion and by March 1919 it had a membership of 260 men. The regiment – or what was left of it numbering about 50 men – returned home for demob towards the end of April via Scotland and Crystal Palace. The colours were returned to Hertford on Wednesday the 23rd April 1919.

Further celebrations and dinners were to follow, unfortunately no lists of those who attended these functions appear to have been recorded or have survived. The Ware Fire Brigade held a dinner at the Coronation Hall on Tuesday the 3rd June for its returning members – it is recorded that one member gave his life. Sergeant Major Abbot of Raynsford Road organised a dinner held at the Drill Hall on the 17th June for the surviving members of the 1st Battalion Hertfordshire Regiment who lived in the town or its immediate neighbourhood. Some 120 men attended including Captain Albert Hawkes, RSM Edward Clarke and Sergeant Hammond. A National Peace Week was held in August when sporting events were held. On Thursday afternoon, the 21st August, some 400 ex-service men from the town marched to a dinner provide by local employers at the Drill Hall. The Hertfordshire Regiment formed an "Old Comrades Association". Dinners were held annually, usually in London at such venues as Andertons Hotel in Fleet Street, but this was probably beyond the means of the rank and file. But it is known that senior NCOs from Ware, such as RQSM Keterer, attended.

The Old Contemptibles Association was also formed with branches throughout the country which enabled the "chums" (as everyone regardless of rank was known) to keep in contact. Ware's "chums" met at the Hertford branch whose secretary at one time was Syd Ditton of Milton Road in Ware. The association helped their comrades who had fallen on hard times and by 1930 were publishing their own magazine which finally ceased publication in December 1975. Social events such as dances were held at the Drill Hall. The "chums" of the Old Contemptibles Association always proudly headed the march past the Cenotaph in Whitehall on Armistice Day.

Chapter 14
THE CROSS OF SACRIFICE

Before the war had ended a general committee had been set up by Ware Urban District Council to consider the provision of a suitable memorial to those who had laid down their lives during the conflict. A sub-committee was formed specifically to look into the proposals for the memorial. Suggestions tabled included:

(i)   A stone memorial with several sites suggested, including Star Street, Rankin Square, the Market Place, the Old Churchyard, Henderson Corner and the Eagle.

(ii) The Vicar proposed that seats were laid out in various parts of the town together with a garden as a pleasure resort.

(iii) Mr Albany suggested that the Council should form a colony of housing and workshops together with recreational rooms for discharged soldiers.

(iv) Mr A H Rogers proposed an Institution to comprise of a free public library and rooms for recreation.

(v)   Mr J Rogers said that he thought that no better scheme could be contemplated than to build almshouses for married couples such as those built and endowed by the Ware Charities – to be allotted in the first instance to wounded or incapacitated soldiers.

The sub-committee sought the advice of Sir Reginald T Bloomfield, one of four architects retained by the War Graves Commission for the design of War Memorials. He recommended that the most suitable site was in the corner of the New Burial Ground i.e. on the north side of Church Street facing Mr Yorke's forge. His proposal was that a 22 foot high cross with a bronze sword set in the centre be mounted on a square platform accessed by three steps. The names of the fallen were to be carved on a tablet at the back and the whole memorial was to be in Portland stone. The cost was estimated at £1000. The committee favoured the Cross of Sacrifice as the permanent memorial to "Our Boys" who had laid down their lives for King and Country.

A public meeting was held in the Town Hall on Monday the 28th April 1919 when the committee described the various suggestions. Their recommendation was that the Cross of Sacrifice located in the New Burial Ground adjacent to the churchyard was the most suitable. A motion proposed by Mr E H Hitch and seconded by Dr A J Boyd that the Committee's proposals be accepted aroused a long and heated debate. A Mr Kielf rose and said he was against the idea of spending £1000 for public property standing on private land – the site proposed was church land. He proposed that no decision be taken that night since he had a petition containing nearly a thousand signatures addressed to Mrs Croft of Fanhams Hall, respectfully asking her to sell or lease the Priory grounds for rest and recreational purposes.

However before all the wrangling and arguments between the various factions of the town had been resolved the Ware Scouts stole the march on everyone and erected a memorial to their comrades who had fallen in the war. This took the form of a roll of honour painted on a board and hung on the church railings where the present memorial stands. Allen and Hanbury followed suit when Captain Capel Hanbury unveiled a brass plaque at their sports pavilion in June 1920 dedicated to the eleven colleagues who made the supreme sacrifice. A list of men who had fallen in the war was also hung in St Mary's Church.

Mrs Croft agreed to let the Priory to the Urban District Council for a period of 90 years (subsequently changed to a 999 year lease) but the argument continued as to where the memorial should be sited. In June 1919 another public meeting was held. The committee still wanted to site the Memorial in the corner of the New Burial Ground and to raise money for its construction by public subscription. This was opposed by a section of the town led by Mr Kielf who proposed that the council obtain the site of Yorke's old forge (the present Memorial Gardens) and build the war memorial there. The meeting became heated and it was even mooted that the relatives of the fallen should have the final say. Needless to say, the site the Memorial remained unresolved that night.

Neither side appear to have done their homework since the so-called New Burial Ground (which had been acquired in 1833 and not been used since 1854) was town property by virtue of the 1852 Burial Act and a precept by the Church Overseers in 1854. However the ground was still consecrated and could not be disturbed without the authority of the Chancellor of the Diocese. At a special Vestry meeting convened by the Vicar of St Mary's, Canon Martin Reed, and his Churchwardens it was agreed to petition the Chancellor for a faculty to erect the proposed War Memorial within the New Burial Ground. Permission was duly granted and Mr Kielf's objections were overcome and the town was not put to the additional expense of buying Mr Yorke's forge.

By November 1919 a list of names which were to be carved on the memorial had been prepared and posted in public places within the town, the public being asked to send corrections to Miss Croft at Fanhams Hall. Since Miss Croft had been the SSFA representative, it sounds as if she prepared the initial list of those killed.

On Sunday afternoon, the 30th January 1921, several thousand people gathered in the vicinity of St Mary's Church in spite of a high winds and a threatening storm to witness the unveiling of the War Memorial. An inter-denominational |service was conducted in the church by Canon Reed before a congregation nearing a thousand people, mainly relatives of the fallen. The Bishop of St Albans was in attendance. Outside the church the band of the newly-formed Beds and Herts Regiment took up the music played on the organ enabling the onlookers to

The Cross of Sacrifice War Memorial being dedicated on a wet Sunday in 1921

partake in the hymns. The regiment also provided a guard of honour. The War Memorial, draped in a huge Union Jack donated by Mrs R B Croft, was unveiled by Viscount Hampden, the Lord Lieutenant for Hertfordshire and former Commanding Officer of the 1st Battalion of the Hertfordshire Regiment. The prayers of dedication were led by the Bishop of St Albans and the last post played by Sergeant Carpenter, followed by an address by Viscount Hampden.

A list of names engraved on the plinth of the Cross of Sacrifice was published with the account of the unveiling in the *Hertfordshire Mercury*. However the list was inaccurate: two men in the "Herts Guards" who were in fact killed were included in the published list but their names do not appear on the War Memorial. In common with many inscriptions on memorials throughout the country the list of names is not definitive. Some names have not been included on the Memorial, simply because their relatives did not wish to be reminded of their loved one's ultimate sacrifice.

After the war the bereaved families were issued with commemorative plaques and citations. Many of the plaques were mounted in a frame by an enterprising gentleman who toured the town – he returned later to do the same with the "Roll of Honour" certificates, but having collected the money neither he nor the certificates were seen again.

The Roll of Honour of "Our Boys" most of whom joined the Herts Guards

They shall not grow old, as
we that are left grow old,
age shall not weary them,
nor the years condemn.
At the going down of the
sun and in the morning
we will remember them.

Laurence Binyon's *For the Fallen*

In the Roll of Honour which follows, where other members of a man's family
served in the forces, brief details have been included under the man's name.

Adams family of 3 Collett Road

Mrs Maria Adams, the widow of Mr Charles Adams who died on the 17th June 1914, had five sons serving in the war three of whom were killed.

Adams C E – 26989 (formerly 2454) Private Charles Edward Adams was a married man, he and his wife Annie lived at 23 The Bourne. Charles enlisted in the Hertfordshire Regiment, probably in August 1914, and joined the 1st Battalion in France during 1916. He was transferred to the 6th Somerset Light Infantry. Charlie was reported as missing and subsequently it was confirmed that he was killed on the 16th September 1916. After his death his wife lived at 3 High Oak Road.

Adams E W – 266562 Private Ernest William Adams was the second of Maria's sons to be killed. Ernest was mortally wounded on Sunday the 23rd September 1917 whilst holding newly won lines at "Shrewsbury Forest" to the south of the Menim Road at Ypres. He was 26 years old. Ernest Adams has no known grave and his name is commemorated at Tyne Cot Memorial at Passchendaele and also appears on the Hatfield War Memorial. A report of his death appeared in the *Mercury* and reads as follows:

Quite a number of casualties occurred among the Herts Territorials at the Front on 23rd-24th September and one of the unfortunate lads to go under was 266562 Private E W Adams. He was the son of Maria Adams of 3 Collett Road Ware and the son-in-law of Mr and Mrs S Wilson of New Town, Hatfield. The last named received a letter from a comrade, Private Herbert Shadbolt, on behalf of the Company expressing their sorrow at losing him as he was a good comrade and a good soldier, always cheerful and bright and willing to do whatever he was asked to do. He was hit by a German shell with his face to the enemy, and suffered no pain. The deceased, who leaves a widow and child, was wounded in the spine in January of this year and was sent out to France again in July.

Adams A T– 28680 Private Alfred Thomas Adams of the Essex Regiment was the third brother to be killed. Again he was a married man with two young children. He had been employed at the Post Office in Ware and before he joined up he was a postman at Great Yarmouth. He was reported missing in April 1917. It was not until September 1918 that his death was confirmed finally ending months of anxiety for his widow. His name is commemorated under the Essex Regiment on the War Memorial.

Who the other two sons in the forces were is not known for certain. It seems likely that A Adams of Collett Road who attended the party at the Drill Hall on the 29th January 1919 was one. Maria died on the 8th March 1944 at the age of 83 and is buried in Ware Cemetery. Her gravestone also commemorates her three sons who died in the war together with another son Richard who died in 1960 aged 65 years – also old enough to have served in the war.

Akers family of New Road

Mr and Mrs George Akers, who ran a shop at 9 New Road, were a family with strong military connections since in November 1914 they had four sons and two grandsons serving in the army. Their eldest son was in the National Reserve, their second son was in the 1st Battalion of the Bedfordshire Regiment, two were in the "Herts Terriers" (Private H Akers went to France in November 1914) and the fifth was in France with the Army Service Corps. The two grandsons were John Robert Akers who was serving with the Royal Fusiliers in Calcutta (where he died) and Gunner George Albert Munt who was in France with the 39th Battery of the Royal Field Artillery.

Akers J F – 26990 (formerly 242) Acting Corporal James Frederick Akers was a married man, he and his wife Nellie lived at 9 New Road. James Akers was a pre-war "Terrier", he took part in the monthly rifle shoots in 1909 and by 1913 he was a Lance Corporal. It is known from his army medal rolls that he did not go to France until 1916. It may be that he had completed his term of engagement prior to the outbreak of war and was the son in the National Reserve. In August 1916 he was accidentally injured in bayonet exercises in France. He was then attached or transferred to the 6th Somerset Light Infantry with whom he was killed in action on the 16th September 1916.

Andrews family of 8 Princes Street

Mr and Mrs Richard Andrews of 8 Princes Street had six sons in the war, four of whom were killed in action. Richard Andrews died on the 29th November 1918 (aged 72 years). In the space of two years Mrs Andrews had lost five of her family.

Andrews Walter – 4785 Private Walter Andrews went to France in 1916 where he served with the 1st Battalion of the Hertfordshire Regiment and died on the 13th November 1916 from the wounds he received at the Battle of Ancre.

Andrews J – 4908 Private John Andrews, the eldest son served in the 1st Middlesex Regiment and was killed in action on the 23rd April 1917. He is commemorated on the War Memorial under the Middlesex Regiment.

Andrews A – 32911 Private Albert Andrews enlisted at Bedford and served with the 1st Battalion Bedfordshire Regiment. He was killed by a shell on the 30th July 1917 as his battalion took over a section of German lines at Arleux near Vimy Ridge. Albert was 19 years old and is commemorated on the War Memorial under the Bedfordshire Regiment.

Andrews W – 203195 (formerly 5485) Private William Andrews was a married man: he and his wife, Primrose, together with their three young children lived next to his parents at 6 Princes Street. He enlisted in the Hertfordshire Regiment and went to France in 1916. He transferred to the Essex Regiment and was killed in action with their 11th Battalion on the 11th April 1917 at the age of 28 years.

Cakebread family

Two soldiers by the name of Cakebread appear on the Ware War Memorial. Where the Cakebread family lived in Ware has not been established. The common link the two soldiers have is with Bengeo and almost certainly means that they were brothers who were born in Ware. It is known that Charles Cakebread had a sister, Mrs Bennet, living at 59 Duncombe Road Bengeo – perhaps their parents had died. It is possible that 266648 (formerly 5057) Private Thomas Cakebread who was wounded in the German Spring Offensive in 1918 was a relation – he was the last of Ware's bargees.

Cakebread Charles E – 235226 (formerly 5618) Private Charles Edward Cakebread enlisted with the Hertfordshire Regiment at Hertford going to France in 1916. At some stage he was transferred to the 17th Battalion Royal Welsh Fusiliers with whom he was killed in action on the 30th August 1918 at the age of 27 years.

Cakebread Ernest J – 36296 (formerly 6018) Private Ernest Cakebread the younger of the two brothers Ernest enlisted in the Hertfordshire Regiment and went to France in 1916. Like many others from Ware he was transferred to the 6th Battalion Royal Berkshire Regiment with whom he was wounded, brought back home and sadly died of his wounds on the 8th October 1916 at the age of 20 years. His final resting place is marked by a War Grave Commission headstone in Bengeo's Holy Trinity Church-yard.

Castle C – 2682 Private Charles Castle was born in Ware and was a married man with three young children: he and his wife lived in West Street. Charles enlisted at Hertford at the end of August 1914. He and his brother Robert went to France with the first group of the "Herts Terriers" and landed at Le Havre on the 6th November 1914. The following day, at No. 2 Rest Camp, he was accidentally shot in the head, possibly through being unfamiliar with the new rifle he was issued with a couple of days before sailing to France.

Clark G – 270491 (formerly 1430) Private George Constantine Clark was born at Stepney and came to live in Ware. George was a drummer in the Territorials before the war and went to France in November 1914. He was discharged on the 8th March 1916, having completed his fixed term of engagement, but rejoined the "Herts Guards" and returned to France on active service. He was killed in action on the 3rd July 1917 at the Hilltop Sector near Ypres.

His brother, 20522 Private **Arthur John Clark** who was also born in London and came to Ware, served in the 2nd Battalion of the Bedfordshire Regiment in France. He was killed in action with the Bedfordshires on the 30th July 1916.

Clark E   MSM – 265147 (formerly 1819) Acting RSM Edward Clark, was born in Ware and lived at 23 New Road. Edward joined the "Terriers" before the war probably at the age of sixteen. He was 23 years old when he was killed on the 24th March 1918 when the 1st Battalion Hertfordshire Regiment was forced to retreat during the German Spring offensive on the Somme. Edward was awarded the Meritorious Service Medal for "devotion to duty" during the retreat. He must have been an exceptional man to achieve the rank he did at such a young age.

Clibbon family of 4 Redan Road, Musley Hill

Eliza Clibbon had two sons killed in action. It is believed that she was married to John Clibbon who was killed serving with the Bedfordshires.

Clibbon H G – G/15567 (formerly 6039) Private Herbert G Clibbon was the third son of Mrs J Clibbon. He joined the Hertfordshire Regiment and was later transferred to the Royal Sussex Regiment with whom he was killed at the Battle of St Julien on the 31 July 1917 aged 25 years.

Clibbon A – 43352 (formerly 4392) Lance Corporal Albert Clibbon was the second son of Mrs J Clibbon to die in the war. He enlisted in the Hertfordshire Regiment and went to France to join the 1st Battalion on the 17th August 1915. Later he was transferred to the 2nd Battalion of the Bedfordshire Regiment, was taken prisoner and died of his wounds in German hands on the 6th June 1918. Albert's name appears on the War Memorial under the Bedfordshire Regiment.

Clibbon J – 4/5173 Private John Clibbon who, although a Ware resident, enlisted in the Bedfordshire Regiment at Hatfield. His army number indicates that he joined their 4th Battalion. Possibly he was in the services prior to the outbreak of war and may well have been Mrs Clibbon's husband. John went to France on the 8th November 1914 and was killed in action with the 1st Battalion of the Bedfordshires on the 18th April 1915. His name does not appear on the War Memorial.

The Cockman family of 25 Crib Street and the Page families of Bowling Road and Crib Street

Mr and Mrs Charles Cockman of 25 Crib Street had a large family of seventeen children and at least two of their sons served in the forces. Their son Richard was killed at the Battle of St Julien.

Cockman R MM – 265264 (formerly 2071) Lance Corporal Richard Cockman was born and lived in Ware. He served with the "Terriers" before the outbreak of the war, going to France with the first group of the 1st Battalion in November 1914. Richard was wounded in the line adjacent to the La Bassée Canal on the 12th March 1915 and was sent to No 2 Stationary Hospital Boulogne. Promoted to Lance Corporal he was wounded again at the Battle of St Julien on the 31st July 1917 – it was here that he gained his Military Medal. Richard Cockman was killed in the front lines in the Voormezeele sector south of Ypres when the Hertfordshires came under very heavy shell fire on the 26th April 1918. Richard has no known grave and his name is commemorated at Tyne Cot Memorial at Passchendaele.

Richard's sister Daisy married 2275 Guardsman **George Page**, the son of Mr and Mrs Alfred Page of 18 Bowling Road. George was a Sunday School teacher at the Congregational Church and he and Daisy lived at 22 Princes Street with their young daughter Kathleen. George enlisted in the Coldstream Guards and was killed on the Somme on the 25th August 1918, aged 28 years. He is buried in the Frevent Cemetery, fifteen miles from the town of Albert. **Richard Page MM** of Bowling Road was probably his brother. After George's death, Daisy married his cousin, Alf Page, the son of Joshua and Elizabeth Page of 32 Crib Street. Alf had served with the Hertfordshire Regiment and was wounded at the Battle of St Julien. Joshua and Elizabeth's youngest son, G/62106 Private **Herbert Page**, enlisted with the East Kent Regiment, went to France on the 8th July 1918 and was killed in action with the 20th

Guardsman George Page with his wife Daisy (née Cockman) and daughter Kathleen (now Mrs Kathleen Sayer).

Battalion Middlesex Regiment on the 20th August 1918, at the age of eighteen. He had been a bandsman in the Ware Salvation Army. He is buried in the Hagle Dump Cemetery some seven miles to the west of Ypres. Alf and Herbert were probably cousins of Walter and Joshua Page of 40 Crib Street, both of whom served with the Hertfordshire Regiment and were wounded.

Crook A J – 265753 (formerly 2944) Private Arthur John Crook was the son of Walter and Lydia Crook of 32 Gladstone Road who came from Battersea to Ware. Three of his brothers were also in the forces. Arthur enlisted at Hertford and went to France with the first draft of the 1st Battalion Hertfordshire Regiment on the 23rd January 1915. He was wounded at the Battle of Festubert. He was subsequently attached to the 4th Battalion of the Bedfordshire Regiment with whom he was again wounded. He was repatriated to England at the end of 1917 and died of wounds at Heathdene Hospital, Harrogate on 22nd September 1918 in his 27th year. Arthur was buried in Ware Cemetery and a Commonwealth War Grave's headstone marks his final resting place.

Three more of Mr and Mrs Crook's sons served with the "Herts Guards". Frederick, their youngest son, went to France in 1914 and rose to the rank of Acting Company Sergeant-Major. He too was wounded at the Battle of Festubert and was captured during the German's Spring Offensive on the Somme in April 1918. Private Ernest Crook was a time-served pre-war Territorial who rejoined at the outbreak of war. He also went to France in 1914 with the 1st Battalion and was invalided home having been wounded in February 1915. Ernest joined up again with the 2/1st Battalion Cambridgeshire Regiment. Their eldest son, Private Walter Crook served with the Oxfordshire and Buckinghamshire Light Infantry in Mesopotamia.

French W J – 15591 Private Walter J French (Jack) was the son of Mr and Mrs French of 46 Bowling Road. He enlisted in the Hertfordshire Regiment but was subsequently transferred to the 12th Battalion Royal Sussex Regiment who were in the 39th Division with the Hertfordshires and would have taken part in the same battles. He was killed in action on the 21st October 1916.

His brother, 267028 Private Charlie French also served in the Hertfordshire Regiment, he was wounded with the 1st Battalion in the Ancre sector in September 1916 and upon recovering was transferred to the Northumberland Fusiliers. He was wounded again in July or August 1917 with his new regiment.

Gosselin A DSO – Captain Alwyn Gosselin was the eldest child of Sir Martin Hadsley Gosselin of Blakesware, Wareside. His father, who died in 1905, had been Assistant Under-Secretary of State for Foreign Affairs and his grandfather, Martin Hadsley Gosselin, had lived in Ware Priory. Alwyn Gosselin enlisted in the Grenadier Guards with whom he won the DSO. He was killed in action in 1915, aged 31 years.

Gray F – 3156 Acting Corporal Frank Gray was born at Richmond and was the adopted son of Mr and Mrs George Game, of 11 Gladstone Road. He enlisted at Hertford and went to France with the first batch of reinforcements on the 23rd January 1915. Frank was killed on the 13th November 1916 during the Battle of the Ancre. Mr and Mrs Game received the following letter from Albert Hawkes, the vocalist, who was with him at the time: "I hardly know how to write and tell you that dear old Frank was killed in action on the morning of the 13th. I am so frightfully busy now, as we are on the move, but when we get settled down I will write and let you know all particulars. All I can say is that I for one have lost one of the best pals I have ever had. His officer told me that he was one of the best men he had on the Lewis guns". Frank Gray was 20 years old when he died.

Gray J T DCM – 266398 (formerly 4549) Private John Gray was the eldest son of Mr and Mrs John Gray of 22 Bowling Road. He enlisted in the Hertfordshire Regiment at Hertford and went to France on the 10th July 1915. John was wounded at the Battle of Ancre. It was here that he gained his Distinguished Conduct Medal, the citation for which read: "For conspicuous gallantry in action. He displayed great courage and initiative when in charge if fourteen enemy prisoners who endeavoured to escape and finally brought them back to Battalion Headquarters". At some stage he was transferred to the Bedfordshire Regiment, possibly after he recovered from his wounds. He was killed on the 6th March 1918 in his 24th year.

Hammond family

Mr and Mrs Herbert Hammond who ran the Cherry Tree pub in Amwell End had two sons killed in the war.

Hammond H J – 265148 (formerly 1820) Sergeant Hiram John Hammond was their younger son. Hiram was married living with his family in Kibes Lane and worked for Hitch the builder. He was a pre-war Territorial and went to France as a Lance Corporal in November 1914 becoming the senior Sergeant in No 3 Company. Hiram was wounded at the Battle of St Julien on the 31st July 1917 and taken to a casualty clearing station which was hit and destroyed by a shell. Initially he was reported as missing, but later it was confirmed that he died on that date at the age of 28 years. Hiram has no known grave and his name is commemorated on the Menim Gate in the town of Ypres.

Hammond H S – 4/7001 Sergeant Herbert (Harold) S Hammond was the elder son. He served with the 4th Battalion Bedfordshire Regiment and was killed in action on November 13th 1916 on the opening day of the Battle of Ancre. His battalion attacked the Germans in thick fog between the River Ancre and Beaumont Hamel. He was 30 years old and like his brother Hiram was a married man with a family – he may have lived at 20 Crib Street. His name appears on the War Memorial under the Bedfordshire Regiment.

Hart Family of 12 Priory Street

John Hart, a captain of one of Ware's many barges, and his wife had a family of fourteen children and lived at 12 Priory Street. At least two of their sons served in the forces.

Hart F H MM   265957 (formerly 3322) Private Frederick Hart was their second son. Before the war he was employed at Mr Minard's nursery in Ware. He enlisted in the Hertfordshire Regiment in August 1914 at Hertford and went to France in 1915 landing there on the 21st January. He was wounded in the arm and leg at St Jean (outside of Ypres) in the Hilltop sector in July 1916 and spent time in the 8th Stationary Hospital France. For his part in the Battle of Ancre on the 13th November 1916 he was awarded the Military Medal. He was wounded again in the early part of 1917 and was subsequently attached to the 1st Battalion Bedfordshire Regiment and transferred to the Italian front where he was wounded on July 18th, dying two days later. His parents heard from his battalion's chaplain that their son had died of wounds to the back with penetration to the lungs and was unconscious for several hours before his death. He was 23 years of age.

Their eldest son, 17328 Private **Benjamin (Bennie) John Hart**, served with the Bedfordshire Regiment during the war. He volunteered for service on the 26th September 1914 and went to France with their 8th Battalion in 1915. He was caught in a gas attack and was discharged with a Silver War Badge on the 26th September 1916 and died of the effects of mustard gas in the 1930s.

Hills H – 28685 Private Henry (Harry) A Hills was one of two sons of Mrs A Hills of 154 Musley Hill who served in the war. Both were bandsmen in the 1st Battalion of the Hertfordshire Regiment. Henry went to France in 1916 and was attached to the Duke of Cornwall's Light Infantry and with this unit that he was killed in action 21st October 1917 in his 21st year.

His brother, 265099 (formerly 1706) Private William T Hills, was in the Territorials before the war as a drummer in the Drum and Fife band. He went to France with the 1st Battalion in November 1914 and was wounded at the Battle of Festubert and again on the 30th March with three bullet wounds in his right foot during the German spring offensive on the Somme in 1918.

Huggins P H – 2701 Private Percy Henry Huggins was the son of Mr and Mrs Huggins, upholsterers of Victoria House, 8 Baldock Street. He was one of the first recruits to enlist at Hertford at the end of August 1914 and went to France with the 1st Battalion of the Hertfordshire Regiment in November 1914. The battalion went up to the Front on the 23rd December and moved into the front line on Christmas Eve. Percy, who was in "D" Company (mainly Watford men), was on sentry duty in a *sap* very close to the German lines and was shot in the head by a sniper. He was buried in a little cemetery near the front line. Following his death, Lance Sergeant Thomas Edward Gregory of Watford who was a crack shot volunteered to shoot the sniper which he did. Gregory was in turn killed by another sniper on the same day. Percy's brother was also in the war.

Johnson H A – 36369 (formerly 5603) Private Henry Alfred Johnson was the son of Mrs Hastler of 45 Trinity Road. Henry enlisted with the Hertfordshire Regiment but transferred to the 6th Battalion Royal Berkshire Regiment with whom he was killed in action in October 1916. His mother received the following letter from his company commander, Lieutenant Barrett: "Private H A Johnson was unfortunately killed by a shell on 31st October. We were occupying the front line at the time and Johnson was one of a fatigue party sent down to battalion headquarters on fatigue. As the party returned at 2 pm Johnson was unfortunately hit. He was buried 20 yards away from the spot where he fell and a large wooden cross marks the place. He was an excellent man in action and we all feel his loss keenly".

Keene G H – 3139 Private George Henry Keene was born in Reading and was the son of Mr Charles Keene, overseer in the Reading Post Office. George came to Ware in June 1913 when he was employed in the office of Mr G H Gisby, the solicitor and also Town Clerk, and he enlisted at Hertford in August 1914 going to France with the first draft in January 1915. He was killed by a grenade in a section of the trenches known as "A1" near Annequin on the 26th October 1915 at the age of 24 years.

Knight F C – 235295 (formerly 7/7214) Private Frederick Charles Knight was the son of Mr Charles Knight, the baker at 10 Crib Street. He enlisted in the Hertfordshire Regiment in 1916 and transferred to the Northumberland Fusiliers with whom he was wounded in December 1916. His army number indicates he initially served with their 7th Battalion. Frederick recovered in hospital at Wrexham, returned to France and was killed in action with their 12th/13th Battalion on the 28th March 1918.

Lee family of 69 Crib Street

William and Jane Lee of 69 Crib Street had at least five sons serving in the forces. William and Walter were with the RAMC, Harry and Philip in the Hertfordshire Regiment and Frederick in the Royal Navy. Two of them were killed.

Lee H – 36381 (formerly 2914) Private Harry Lee enlisted in the Hertfordshire Regiment and went to France with the 1st Battalion in November 1914. He was transferred to the 2nd Battalion Royal Berkshire Regiment as a Lewis gunner and was killed by a shell on the 27th April 1918.

Lee P C – 36384 (formerly 5696) Private Philip Charles Lee followed his brother Harry into the Hertfordshire Regiment. He too transferred to the Royal Berkshire Regiment where he saw service with their 6th Battalion as a driver. Philip died of wounds on the 17th August 1917 at 32 Casualty Clearing Station in France. He was 24 years old.

Martin C – 4593 Private Charles Martin was the second son of Mr and Mrs George Martin of 9 Princes Street. He enlisted in the Hertfordshire Regiment at Hertford and went to France on the 10th July 1915. Charles was killed at the Battle of Ancre on the 13th November 1916. Sergeant W G Butler (possibly his platoon sergeant) wrote to his mother: "It is with deep regret that I am writing to inform you that Charlie lost his life in Monday's great battle. He was mortally wounded by a German officer when doing splendid work in the German trenches, but we were all pleased to hear that he was quickly avenged by a comrade who promptly accounted for the officer. Although Charlie received prompt attention and every care, he passed away soon afterwards on the battlefield. I cannot express how deeply we, his comrades, all deplore his loss, for he was a splendid fellow, carried out all his duties, whether in or out of the trenches, to the best of his ability and he could always be relied upon when placed in a dangerous post. We shall all miss him, for he has been with us so long, but we must console ourselves with the knowledge that no longer will he have to suffer the dangers and trials that we are still enduring. May God comfort you in this time of grief and help you to bear your burden with fortitude. Just before going into action Charlie promised to sell a German helmet to our Medical Officer, so I am enclosing the money he would have received for it in this letter, trusting you will receive it safely". (Charlie was shot while escorting a party of German prisoners back from the Front; the German Officer was promptly "despatched" by Private John Gray – see notes on the Battle of Ancre.)

Martin E – 266608 Private Ernest Martin was a married man who lived at 154 Musley Hill. He enlisted in the Hertfordshire Regiment and was wounded with the 1st Battalion at the Battle of St Julien on the 31st July 1917. Ernest was transferred or attached to the 3rd Battalion Bedfordshire Regiment, presumably after he recovered from his injuries, and it was with this Regiment when he was killed in action on the 27th August 1918.

Martin T F – 265149 (formerly 1821) Acting Sergeant Thomas Frederick Martin was the son of Mr and Mrs Martin of 7 London Road. Thomas was a pre-war Territorial in "C" Company based at the Drill Hall at Amwell End and went to France in November 1914. He was killed in the Voormezeele sector near Ypres on the 26th April 1918 during the Third Battle of Lys. Thomas Martin was 26 years old and has no known grave – his name is commemorated at Tyne Cot Memorial at Passchendaele.

Newman F DCM – 2224 Sergeant Frank Newman was born in Ware, the son of James Newman, a gardener, and his wife Jennie. The family moved to London and Frank was employed by a manufacturing chemist and later apprenticed to a saw piercer. He joined the London Regiment (TF) in 1905, went to Malta with them on the outbreak of war and then to France in January 1915. At the Battle of Neuve Chapelle in March 1915 he was awarded the DCM for conspicuous gallantry in encouraging his men though wounded in a charge on the enemy trenches. After recovering in London, he rejoined his regiment and was again wounded and died in hospital on the 2nd September 1915, in his twenty-third year. He is buried at Merville Cemetery.

Newman J O – 36413 (formerly 6147) Lance Sergeant Joseph Oliver Newman of 11 Bowling Road, enlisted with the Hertfordshire Regiment and was transferred to the 6th Battalion Royal Berkshire Regiment with whom he was killed in action on the 31st July 1917. In a letter to his widow Captain J N Richardson said: "I'm very grieved to tell you that your husband was killed in action on Tuesday morning, 31st July during the big attack near Ypres. The company was advancing near a wood called Glenourse when your brave husband was shot and died within five minutes so he did not suffer pain. He was a gallant and smart soldier and I feel his loss very much." (Glencorse Wood was about two miles to the east of Hooge). Sergeant Newman was killed on the opening day of this battle when so many other men from

The Roll of Honour plaque and the Distinguished Conduct Medal awarded to Sgt Frank Newman, a Territorial soldier, for "conspicuous gallantry" at Neuve Chapelle on the 10th March 1915. Although wounded he continued to encourage his men and after the battle said to his colonel: "They won't call us Saturday night soldiers now, Sir."

the town died. His name is commemorated on the War Memorial under the Berkshire Regiment.

Newton family of 71 Star Street

Mrs Newton suffered as much anguish as Mrs Andrews of Princes Street and Maria Adams of Collett Road. Mrs Newton was the widow of Joseph Newton who died in 1909; she remarried to Richard Presland and lost a son, a son-in-law and two step-sons during the war.

Newton H D – 39638 (formerly 2516) Sergeant Harold Douglas Newton was a married man whose wife lived at 17 Townsend Street in Hertford. Harold went to France with the 1st Battalion of the Hertfordshire Regiment in November 1914. At some stage, probably in 1916, he was transferred to the 4th Battalion of the Gloucestershire Regiment with whom he was reported wounded and missing and later confirmed as killed on the 20th September 1917.

Two other sons Corporal Benjamin William Newton (of Cherrytree Yard) and Private Joseph C Newton were both pre-war "Terriers", their army numbers show that they joined on the same day. Both were "Old Contemptibles" with the 1st Battalion of the Hertfordshire Regiment. A fourth son, Ethelbert Thomas Newton, had been a Drummer in the "Terriers" but died in tragic circumstances in March 1914.

Riddle J – 50981 Private James Riddle was Mrs Newton's son-in-law and was killed in action with the Manchester Regiment on the 14th December 1917. The Riddle family lived at Musley Hill.

Newton J G – 3419 Private John George Newton was the 17 year old youngest son of Mr and Mrs John Newton of 6 Chapel Yard, Amwell End. John was killed in action while in the trenches north-east of Vermelles on the 21st November 1915, some three months after arriving in France on the 17th August 1915. His parents received a sincere letter from Captain Hanbury Pawle, the CO of No 3 Company, which said: "It is my sad duty to inform you that your son, No 3419 Private J G Newton was killed when on duty in the trenches this morning. He was shot through the head, and I do not believe that he suffered any pain at all as he died almost instantaneously. It is the saddest of all my duties having to inform those at home of the death of those they have most nobly and unselfishly sent to the Front. I know how difficult it is to see anything but the blackest side when bad news like this comes, but later when one can think about it quietly it is easier to appreciate what a fine thing it is to have lived to come out and lay down one's life for King and country and for the greatest cause that ever man fought for – I mean the cause of freedom. However heavy the blow falls on you, you will be feeling proud of your son now. He was only with me a very short time, but he had many friends in the company, and we all including myself wish to send you our deepest sympathy in your great loss".

Mr and Mrs Newton may have had another son serving as a regular soldier in the Royal Fusiliers who was wounded in France during the retreat from Mons in 1914.

Parrott E A – 242133 (formerly 3120) Private Edward A Parrott enlisted in the Hertfordshire Regiment going to France in 1916. He was transferred to the Gloucestershire Regiment with a new regimental number of 5929 and was killed in action with the 2/5th Battalion on the 13th September 1918. Edward is commemorated on the War Memorial under the Gloucestershire Regiment.

Parnell family of 6 Cross Street

John and Hannah Parnell of 6 Cross Street were yet another family to lose three sons during the war.

Parnell H C – 269399 (formerly 9369) Private Harry Charles Parnell, their youngest son, enlisted in the Essex Regiment before being transferred to the 1st Battalion of the Hertfordshire Regiment. He was reported missing and then confirmed as killed at St Julien on the 31st July 1917 during the Third Battle of Ypres. Harry was 22 years old when he died. Harry has no known grave and is commemorated on the Menin Gate at Ypres.

Parnell J A – 28428 Private John (Jack) Arthur Parnell was Mr and Mrs Parnell's eldest son. He served in the 10th Battalion Essex Regiment and was reported missing and afterwards reported killed on the 26th September 1916. Like his brother Harry he has no known grave and is commemorated on the Thiepval Memorial (Somme Sector). His name appears on the Ware Memorial under the Essex Regiment.

No. *W.H./C264* Rev. 836/8

ARMY FORM B. 104—82.

(In replying, please
quote above No.)

No. 2 Infantry Record Office,
Staines Road, Hounslow. Record Office,

28ᵗʰ August, 1918

Madam,

It is my painful duty to inform you that a report has been received from the War Office notifying the death of:—

(No.) *G. 38702* (Rank) *Private*

(Name) *Alfred William Parnell.*

(Regiment) *Royal West Kent*

which occurred *41 Casualty Clearing Station, France*

on the *23rd August, 1918.*

The report is to the effect that he *died of wounds*

By His Majesty's command I am to forward the enclosed message of sympathy from Their Gracious Majesties the King and Queen. I am at the same time to express the regret of the Army Council at the soldier's death in his Country's service.

I am to add that any information that may be received as to the soldier's burial will be communicated to you in due course. A separate leaflet dealing more fully with this subject is enclosed.

I am,

Mrs A. Parnell.
146, Musley Hill,
Ware,
Herts.

Madam,

Your obedient Servant,

Officer in charge of Records.

18540. Wt. 6529/M 2529. 150m. 7/17. R. & L., Ltd. Forms B 104—82/2.

P.T.O.

The dreaded letter received by the wife of Private Alfred William Parnell in 1918 – two of his brothers were killed in 1916 and 1917.

Parnell A W – G/38072 Private Alfred William Parnell was a married man with a young son living at 146 Musley Hill. Alfred served with the 7th Battalion Royal West Kent Regiment. He died at No 41 Casualty Clearing Station at Daours from wounds received on the 23rd August 1918 and was buried in the Communal Cemetery established there. Daours is a few miles east of Amiens and the cemetery has a commanding view over the Somme Valley. He is commemorated on the Ware Memorial under the West Kent Regiment.

Mysterious deaths en route for India

John and Hannah's daughter, Lily, married Henry King who served in the 1st Battalion of the Hertfordshire Regiment. Henry, whose parents lived in a cottage near the Ware Viaduct, enlisted at the age of twenty one on the 9th September 1914 and went to France with the first draft in November 1914. At some stage he suffered in a gas attack. He was lucky to be alive after the Ancre operations in November 1916 since he was reported missing and found several days later buried up to his armpits in the Somme mud. Henry came back to England to recover and was due for discharge. However, against the wishes of his family, he reported back to his unit and joined the newly formed 2nd Garrison Battalion of the Bedfordshires. The Garrison Battalion was raised on the 27th December 1916 and comprised of men who were over age or unfit for service in active areas. As soon as it was up to strength (and unbeknown to his family) he left for India in March 1917, on the *Orontes*, travelling via Sierra Leone to Cape Town or Durban, from where they travelled on an unknown boat to Karachi. The next time Henry's relatives heard from him was from India where his battalion arrived in May. Henry told his family that men were killed on the voyage from Durban to Karachi by a German agent, such was the panic aboard that he with others hid in the engine room. As fantastic as this story may seem research has shown that six members of his battalion died at sea a few days before docking at Karachi on the 6th May. Henry's unit was posted to the Karachi Brigade although exactly where he was located is unknown. He contracted malaria on the sub-continent which lead to his discharge from the Army through ill health with a "Silver War Badge" on the 10th July 1919. He suffered from the effects of gas for the rest of his life. After his "demob" he resumed work at Allan and Hanbury. Two of Henry King's brothers, William (Billy) and Alfred (Alf), also served in the "Herts Guards",

Presland   There were several families by the name of Presland living Ware and the name figured prominently in the town's casualty lists.

Presland family of 17 Coronation Road

Mr and Mrs William Presland of 17 Coronation Road had three sons serving in the forces, one of whom was killed while another survived three serious woundings and returned to his old work in the maltings.

Presland G – 2720 Private George Presland was probably the G Presland whose name appears in the pre-war Territorials shooting competitions as early as 1911. He re-enlisted at Hertford at the outbreak of war. George went to France with the original contingent of the 1st Battalion in November 1914. At some stage, possibly after the Battle of Festubert, he was attached to the 8th Battalion Gloucestershire Regiment with whom he was killed in action on the 30th July 1916. George has no known grave and is commemorated on panel 135 of the Loos Memorial.

The maltmaker who joked and survived

Two more of Mr and Mrs Presland's sons served in the forces. Their son William was born on the 1st January 1887 and joined the Territorials on the 8th April 1908 with a Regimental number of 292. Before the war he was employed as a maltmaker (his photograph appears in *Ware's Past in Pictures* together with a group of eight other of his fellow workers). Bill went to France with the 1st Battalion Hertfordshire Regiment in November 1914 together with his brother George. He was seriously wounded in 1915 during the Battle of Festubert when he was caught in cross fire from machine guns and received bullets in both legs and his nose. He was carried back to a dressing station by a comrade who lived in Amwell End. In his book *Twenty Two Months Under Fire* Brigadier Henry Page Croft described how he sent the men from his old company, the Ware Company, over the top to reinforce the Irish Guards who were in serious difficulties and had suffered major casualties. He knew every man from his home town and it is obvious that most of the men were long serving "Terriers". Page Croft watched as the Herts wounded returned. To quote from his book, "on a stretcher I espied a man who had served under me many years in the time of peace. He was the wag of the company, and his waggishness led several times to slight insubordination, he had appeared before me in the orderly room. Now, as he lay face down on the stretcher and saw me, a roguish look entered his eyes and his pale face lit up as he said, 'well sir I shan't worry you any more; that will be a relief to you in the orderly room'. I saw he was in frightful pain, and I confess a prayer that he might be spared to cause me endless orderly rooms. I remembered that half an hour before I had heard him cheering on his mates with ridiculous jokes as he climbed over the top". That man was Bill Presland. Page Croft obviously did not think Bill would survive since he sent for his brother George to be with him. But the CO's prayers were answered, Bill survived and by the 2nd June he was back in hospital at Birkenhead on the way to recovery.

Once he was discharged from hospital Bill was posted to the 3/1st Battalion at Halton Park, Tring where he remained until he was discharged on the 7th April 1916 having completed his eight year term of engagement with the Territorials. It is interesting to note that his old company commander, Henry Page Croft had not entered Bill's "orderly room" misdemeanours in his military records!

By now conscription to the forces had been introduced and Bill did not wait to become a conscript. He enlisted at Hertford on the 26th July 1916 as 150921 Gunner

William Presland, initially in the Royal Field Artillery and subsequently transferring to the Royal Horse Artillery. He was soon to return to France but before he did so he was to marry into the Tillcock family of Musley Hill (his brother-in-law, 12348 Private **Henry Tillcock**, was killed on the 28th April 1917 with the 6th Battalion Bedfordshire Regiment). In France it appears that Bill spent most of his time taking supplies to the Front. On one occasion he stopped a team of runaway horses towing a limber from crossing a railway line (probably one of the light railways built by the Royal Engineers) and discovered that the driver had been shot.

In the autumn of 1917 he was seriously wounded again on the Ypres front with the 298th Brigade – he had taken supplies to the front lines and came under shell fire. Shrapnel from a gas shell hit his leg, he lost two inches from his shin and was also gassed. Bill spent many months in St Thomas's Hospital in London and was finally discharged from the army on the 6th June 1919 with a Silver War Badge which entitled him to a War Pension of sixteen shillings a week for himself, four shillings for his wife and three shillings for his young daughter. After his discharge he returned to work in the maltings with Gripper Son and Wightman as a sack mender at the Canons Maltings in Baldock Street. When asked by his eldest daughter if he was bitter about the war and his wounds his reply was "I came back, millions didn't". He died in 1961 aged 74.

Mr and Mrs Presland's third son in the forces was 16395 Private Ernest Presland. He served with the 8th Battalion Bedfordshire Regiment arriving in France on the 30th August 1915 and was later posted to Italy.

Presland family of 71 Star Street

Reference has already been made to Mrs Newton who married Richard Presland, two of whose sons were killed in the war.

Presland J – 36418 (formerly 5978) Private John Presland enlisted with the Hertfordshire Regiment but was to transfer to the 6th Battalion Royal Berkshire Regiment. John probably went to France in 1916 and was killed in action on the 29th September 1916.

Presland G – 16790 Sergeant George Presland was the second son to be killed in action. He went to France on the 30th August 1915 in the same draft as Ernest Presland above to join the 8th Battalion Bedfordshire Regiment. George was killed on the 3rd December 1917 on the Somme battlefield in the vicinity of the St Quentin Canal near Gouzeaucourt. He is commemorated on the War Memorial under the Bedfordshire Regiment.

A third son, AB Seaman Richard Presland, served in HMS Kala.

Presland Family of 62 Baldock Street

Mr and Mrs B Presland had at least two sons serving in the forces, their eldest son, 266425 (formerly 4586) Private Sydney Presland of the Hertfordshire Regiment was taken as a prisoner of war at the Battle of St Julien on the 31st July 1917.

A second son, 36419 (formerly 4596) Lance Corporal George Presland enlisted in the Hertfordshire Regiment on the 23 June 1915. He was transferred to the Royal Berkshire Regiment with whom he reported wounded and missing between March 22nd and April 2nd 1918. It is assumed that he was badly wounded and taken prisoner by the Germans since he was in receipt of a Silver War Badge when he was discharged from the army on the 1st April 1919.

Presland Family of Buryfield Terrace

6194 Private J Presland joined Hertfordshire Regiment and transferred to the Royal Fusiliers with whom he was wounded on April 10th 1917, necessitating the amputation of his right leg.

Prior T H – 28698 Private Thomas Prior was employed at French's Mill in Viaduct Road before he enlisted in the Hertfordshire Regiment. He and his wife Dora lived at 2 Cross Street. Thomas transferred to the Duke of Cornwall's Light Infantry and died of his wounds on the battlefield on the 16th September 1916 before he could be taken to an advanced dressing station.

Reynolds G A MM – 265712 (formerly 2865) Sergeant George Albert Reynolds was born in Putney and came to Ware to live in London Road. He enlisted with the "Herts Terriers" in August 1914 and went to France with the original draft on the 5th November of that year. As Corporal George Reynolds he won the Military Medal with the 1st Battalion during the Battle of Ancre in November 1916. He was killed in action at St Julien on the 31st July 1917.

Robinson P – 2636 Private Philip James Robinson was the only son of Mr and Mrs Robert Robinson of 75 New Road. Philip, known as "Buff", was a Sunday School teacher at St Mary's and a member of the choir. He joined the Territorial Force at Hertford with the first group of volunteers a few weeks after war broke out. "Buff" went to France in November 1914 and was the first member of the 1st Battalion Hertfordshire Regiment to be killed in action. He met his death by shell fire on the 18th November 1914 whilst his "C" Company rested outside Ypres having just come out of the front line. His parents received the following letter from Major Page Croft, the Commanding Officer of "C" Company: "I deeply regret to have to inform you that Private Robinson lost his life from the effects of a German shell yesterday, November 18th. His death was instantaneous, and he could not have suffered pain. He was a splendid young fellow, full of pluck and good spirits, and having known him for so many years I feel his loss keenly. He was the first of our Regiment to die for his country, and I trust it may be a small consolation to you to know that he won the esteem of all officers and men, and that his devotion to duty was an example to his countrymen. Believe me, yours in deepest sympathy – H.P.Croft, Major." "Buff" Robinson was 22 years old when he died.

Salmons C H – 265374 (formerly 2287) Private Charles Salmons of 4 New Hill Cottages was born in Ware and was a pre-war "Terrier" who went to France in November 1914. He was reported missing after the Battle of St Julien and it was subsequently confirmed that he was killed in action 31st July 1917.

Saunders T C – 265937 Private Thomas Charles Saunders was the son of Mr and Mrs George Saunders of 1 Willow Wharf, Viaduct Road. He joined the Hertfordshire Regiment at Hertford and had for about two years been acting as a musketry sergeant instructor at a training centre in England. After the disaster at St Julien he volunteered to go out to France as a private and was killed very shortly afterwards on the 21st September 1917 in the support lines at Bugler Wood near Hollebeke to the south of the infamous Ypres–Menim Road.

Savage family of Church Street

Mr and Mrs Arthur Savage of 23 Church Street had two sons killed.

Savage F T – 266789 Lance Corporal Francis Thomas Savage was their eldest son, a married man whose wife's name was Lily. He enlisted on the 6th July 1915 in the Hertfordshire Regiment and was discharged on the 10th January 1919, since he was awarded the Silver War Badge it means that he was discharged through wounds received in the war. He died at home on the 22nd March 1919 after a long and painful illness at the age of 42 years and is buried in Ware Cemetery, his grave being marked with a Commonwealth War Graves Commission headstone.

Savage F C – 6402 Lance Corporal Frederick C Savage was the second son of Arthur Savage to die in the war. He enlisted in the Hertfordshire Regiment going to France in 1916 and was wounded soon after he landed, probably in May. Upon recovery he was transferred to the Essex Regiment, with a regimental number of 43168, and was killed in action with their 10th Battalion on the 23rd March 1918. His name appears on the War Memorial under the Bedfordshire Regiment which is clearly in error and is in conflict with the medal indices held at the Public Records Office.

Shadbolt W R – 235272 (formerly 5503) Private William R Shadbolt of 26 London Road and formerly of 3 Ash Street, Hertford, enlisted with the Hertfordshire Regiment with whom he went to France in 1916. He was subsequently attached or transferred to the Lincolnshire Regiment. It was with the "Lincolnshire Poachers" that he died of wounds received on the 16th August 1917.

Skipp family of 61 New Road

Mr and Mrs Samuel Skipp of 61 New Road had at least four sons serving in the war, one was killed and three were wounded. All four joined the Hertfordshire Regiment but were attached to the Royal Sussex Regiment.

Skipp E – 5703 Private Ernest J Skipp was mortally wounded with the Royal Sussex Regiment, probably in the vicinity of the Schwaben Redoubt in the Ancre Valley, on the 29th October 1916. He died the next day. His brother, Private T W Skipp, was with him when he died.

The second son, 15643 Private Thomas Walter Skipp, was wounded during the Battle of Ancre in November 1916 while on attachment to the Royal Sussex. He was wounded for a second time on the 31st July 1917 during the Battle of St Julien with a bayonet wound in the left leg, he recovered from this in Canterbury Hospital. Thomas returned to France only to be wounded for a third time during the German Spring Offensive on the Somme in March 1918. The third son, 5702 Private Robert Skipp was also wounded at the Battle of Ancre in November.1916.

Their eldest son, 5704 Private Harry Skipp, also transferred to the Royal Sussex Regiment where he was promoted to the rank of Lance Corporal. He took a Commission and joined the Bedfordshire Regiment. In March 1918 Harry was in hospital at Hove suffering from shell shock and fever. He ended the war serving in the Labour Corps.

Smith family of 4 Croft Road

Mrs Annie Smith was another lady who lost both her husband and at least one son during the war – neither death was reported in the local press.

Smith A E – 3596 Private Albert Edward Smith came to Ware from St Albans. Albert enlisted in the Hertfordshire Regiment at the county town and died of sickness at home on the 9th May 1915 aged 45 years. He is buried in Ware Cemetery together with his son J/18802 Able Seaman **Percy Edward Smith** of HMS Renown who died on 24th January 1919 at the age of 22 years. Their Commonwealth War Graves Commission's headstone is unusual since it is marked with two names – both are commemorated on the War Memorial.

Smith A E – 33768 Private Arthur Edward Smith was born in Ware and enlisted at

Hertford. He was killed in action with the 2nd Battalion Bedfordshire Regiment on the 20th September 1917, possibly in a raid on the German trenches at Estaminet Corner near Wytchaete south of Ypres. Since there are no reports in the local paper of his death it could well be that he was the son of Albert Edward Smith above.

Smith Family of 145 Musley Hill

Smith E G – 1826 Private Edward Smith was the son of Mr and Mrs William Smith of 145 Musley Hill. This Smith family probably came to Ware from Stanstead Abbotts. Edward was a pre-war Territorial who had enlisted in the Hertfordshire Regiment at Ware circa 1911. He was among the first of the 1st Battalion to go to France on the 5th November 1914 and was killed in action on the 30th October 1916 in the lines at Schwaben Redoubt just prior to the Battle of the Ancre.

Smith Family of 2 Century Road

Mr and Mrs Smith had three sons serving in the war two of whom laid down their lives.

Smith A E – 36456 (formerly 6148) Private Albert Edward Smith joined the Herts Regiment and was subsequently transferred to the 6th Battalion Royal Berkshire Regiment with whom he was wounded late in 1916 and killed in action on the 12th February 1917.

Smith W H – 5084 Private William Henry Smith enlisted in the Hertfordshire Regiment at the county town either late in 1915 or early 1916. He was killed in action on the 9th July 1916 in the Givenchy-Cuinchy lines near Festubert.

Their third son in the forces was 2583 Private Arthur Smith, a pre-war Territorial with the Hertfordshires, who was wounded at the Battle of Ancre. Following his recovery he was transferred to the Eastern Command Labour Centre of the Labour Corps.

Stamp J – 2528 Corporal Joseph Henry Stamp was born in Ware and was one of "the old brigade" having been a volunteer and Territorial for some eight or nine years prior to the outbreak of war. He was the eldest son of Mr and Mrs Joseph Stamp of 11 Caroline Court, Baldock Street. Joseph Stamp went to France with the 1st Battalion Hertfordshire Regiment on the 5th November 1914 and was wounded in the Battle of Festubert in 1915. He was killed in action at the Battle of Ancre on the 14th November 1916. His company commander, Lieutenant Gallo, writing to his parents described the circumstances of his death: "The Germans made an attack on the position our Company (No 3 Coy) was holding. Your son keeping a good hold on his men, bombed and fired upon the enemy, inflicting heavy loss on them. Two unfortunate

Germans happened to come right up to the post. He killed one man, but the other being desperate shot him through the head. He did some splendid work, and would have been decorated had he survived the attack. It may be of some comfort to you to know that the German who killed your son was himself killed a few minutes later". At the time of his death he was in his 30th year.

Mr and Mrs Stamp had another son in the army, 7051 Private Henry Stamp who served with the 1/5th Battalion Bedfordshire Regiment in Egypt and was wounded twice. A third son, V Stamp, served in the Royal Navy.

Suckling J L – 207098 Private Joseph Suckling was a married man of 45 Baldock Street and the son of Mr and Mrs Joseph Suckling of 8 Blue Coat Yard. Before the war he was employed by Allen and Hanbury, he was in the Territorials as a drummer with the Drum and Fife band at Amwell End. Joseph did not join the 1st Battalion of the Hertfordshire Regiment in France until 1916, presumably he had served his time as a "Terrier" before the outbreak of war. At the time he was killed in action on the 5th October 1917 he was on attachment to the Queen's Royal West Surrey Regiment. His wife received a letter of sympathy from his company commander, Captain H B Secretan, written from Lady Brassey Hospital, Upper Grosvenor Street where Captain Secretan was lying wounded. He wrote: "I am most awfully sorry for your great loss. I could not write before, as I have only just heard the news from the company myself, and I was amongst the first to be wounded. Your husband was a great favourite in the company, and we all used to love to see him play football, he was such a good player and a fine runner too. He was very keen, I know, to get back to his own regiment (the Herts), but we could not manage it for him. He was excellent at his work, and he used to act as an orderly or runner – one who carries messages. I am sorry to say that on October 4th this turned out to be a dangerous job, as the shelling was very heavy. I am afraid I can give you no particulars, but no doubt you have heard from other officers and friends."

Sweeney Family of London Road

Mrs Elizabeth Annie Sweeney of 13 London Road lost both her husband and son during the war. The Sweeneys were related through marriage to Sergeant William Hart of Crib Street.

Sweeney J – Her husband, 3/8632 Private John Sweeney, was of Irish descent and his relatives ran a Marine Store Dealers in The Bourne. He enlisted at Hertford at the age of 45 in the Bedfordshire Regiment after his son Claud went to France. It is said that he chose the Beds since his new comrades would not know his age which suggests that he was not exactly truthful with the Recruiting Sergeant. His army number indicates that initially he was in the 3rd Battalion. He landed in France on the 24th September 1915 and was killed in action a month later at St Jean, some two miles east

Acting Lance Corporal Claud Sweeney MM, who enlisted in the Hertfordshire Regiment at the under age when only 17. He was awarded the Military Medal for gallantry during the Battle of Ancre. He fell in the Battle of St Julien on 31st July 1917, a few days after attaining his 20th birthday.

of the town of Ypres, on the 29th October 1915 with the 8th Battalion Bedfordshire Regiment. He is buried in the White House Cemetery near the village of Jean, probably where he fell since his headstone reads "Known to be buried in this Cemetery".

Sweeney C J W MM – Her son, 265502 (formerly 2537) Private (Acting Lance Corporal) Claud James William Sweeney enlisted in the Hertfordshire Regiment at the age of 17 at Hertford. He was an athletic lad known for diving into the Lea from the Toll Bridge. Claud landed in France on the 23rd of January 1915. In November 1916 he was awarded the Military Medal for gallantry during the Battle of Ancre. He fell in the Battle of St Julien on 31st July 1917, a few days after attaining his 20th birthday, and within a couple of miles of where his father laid down his life. Company Sergeant Major Edward Clarke, a near neighbour of Mrs Sweeney, wrote to her with the sad news of the death of "poor old Claud" as he affectionately calls him. He says he was given the chance to stay out of the attack, but he stoutly refused. "I was with him a few hours before his death, he was then in the very best of spirits and was with his platoon joining in the singing. It was such a shame to lose such a fine chap, and I am sure the few of us who came out of the attack join with me in expressing our sympathy with you in your sad loss, which is ours also." Both Claud Sweeney and Edward Clarke were in No. 3 Company.

Mrs Sweeney was presented with her son's Military Medal at Balls Park, Hertford on the 12th February 1918 by Major Sir H J Delves Broughton, the Commander of the NCOs School there. The Commandant told her how pleased he was to have the honour of presenting her son's decoration to her although he sincerely regretted that he had lost his life in the defence of his country. Three rousing cheers were given by the 450 trainee NCOs who paraded before the medal recipient. Like many others killed at St Julien Claud has no known grave and he is commemorated on the Menin Gate.

Mrs Sweeney's son, Richard Baldock, also served in the "Herts Guards", he was a pre-war Territorial going to France in November 1914.

The Trundle family of 9 Musley Lane

Mr and Mrs Arthur Trundle of 9 Musley Lane had four sons serving in the war one of whom was killed in action.

Trundle J W – 291325 Private James W Trundle joined the Hertfordshire Regiment on the 14th October 1914. In 1916 he joined the 1st Battalion in France where he remained for some months before returning to England through ill health. In October 1916 he was transferred to the 8th Battalion Gloucestershire Regiment with whom he was engaged on coastal works in England until August 1917 when he returned to France only to be killed in action by a shell on the 15th December 1917. He was a married man with one child.

Their son 266642 (formerly 5048) Private Solomon Trundle served with the Herts Regiment in France where he was wounded at the Battle of Ancre in November 1916. He was subsequently transferred to the Bedfordshire Regiment. Solomon was a married man living at 7 Church Alley. A third son, P/4095207 Sergeant George Trundle, was in the Army Service Corps and served in a Base Depot in Egypt while the fourth son 33030 Sergeant Richard Trundle saw service with the 1st Battalion of the Welsh Regiment in Salonica.

Walsingham J – 266008 Sergeant James Walsingham lived at 6 Amwell End with his wife and eight children. He was the eldest son of Mr James Walsingham of Stanstead Abbots and was born at Hertford. He was a hairdresser at Wellington Street in Hertford prior to enlisting in the Hertfordshire Regiment in October 1914. He went to France in 1916, probably with James Trundle above. At the onset of the German's Spring offensive James Walsingham was reported wounded and missing. This was on the 23rd March 1918 during the 1st Battalion's retreat towards the village of Cléry, where it dug in and defended a line of trenches behind the village. It was not until late in May that his wife received a post card from him to say he was a prisoner of war at Limberg and was ill. He died of his wounds as a POW at the 61st Bavarian Hospital on the 28th June 1918 and was buried in the Municipal cemetery at Le Gueany.

Warby E W – 266276 (formerly 4305) Private Ernest William Warby was the son of Mr and Mrs Warby of Bakers End, Wareside, and also 169 Musley Hill. He joined the colours at Hertford early in November 1914 and went to France on the 10th July 1915. He returned home for a weeks leave in February 1916. Ernest was reported missing after the Battle of Ancre on the 13th November 1916 and it was not until March 1917 that he was officially reported as killed on that date.

Wilbourne A H – 266230 (formerly 4193) Sergeant Arthur Herbert Wilbourne lived at 57 High Oak Road with his wife Emily and five children. He enlisted at Hertford and landed in France as a Lance Corporal on the 17th August 1915. Arthur was wounded at the Battle of Ancre in November 1916 by which time he had risen through the ranks to a Sergeant. He was killed in action during the retreat by the 1st Battalion in face of German Spring Offensive in March 1918, probably on the 30th March. At the time of his death he was Acting Company Sergeant-Major. Lieutenant Knee acquainting the widow of his death said: "About five minutes before he was killed he came to me and told me that the No 3 company commander had been killed. This was the last I saw of a very gallant and noble soldier. A splendid man in all respects, always courageous and cheerful in the trenches he gained the respect and admiration of the whole Company". No 3 company commander at the time was probably Captain T P Gibbons. Lieutenant H J Knee was to lose a leg a few days later: in a letter he wrote to the Mercury he said: "The poor battalion was in it right from the start and suffered heavily, how any of us managed to get out alive God only knows".

Members of the 1st Battalion Hertfordshire Regiment killed in action who had family connections in Ware but whose names do not appear on the War Memorial

Clibbon J A – 265367 (Formerly 2273) Private Joseph Abram Clibbon *(photographed right)* was born in Ware in 1896, being the only son of Mr and Mrs Joseph Clibbon of 1 Francis Road. He had nine sisters. Joseph was a pre-war "Terrier" and went to France with the original contingent on the 5th November 1914. During the cold winter of 1914/1915 he suffered frostbite in both his feet and was returned home to recover. He was wounded in the early part of 1916 and was reported to be missing after the Battle of Ancre – it was confirmed later that he had in fact been killed on the 13th November 1916. The sad fact is that he should have been home on leave during the Battle of Ancre but instead allowed a comrade to return to get married.

Jackson E – 2276 L/Corporal Ernest Jackson of 3 Kibes Lane was another pre-war Territorial who went to France with the 1st Battalion in November 1914. He died of the wounds he received in the Battle of Ancre on the 21st November 1916.

Skinner J A – 265518 (formerly 2568) Corporal James Skinner was born in Ware and was an old Ware Territorial, having enlisted in 1908 and completed his time in 1911. He rejoined his regiment immediately the war broke out and went to France with the 1st Battalion on the 5th November. James was killed in action at St Julien on the 31st July 1917. He was the son of Mrs Vernon of Holywell Hill, St Albans

Taylor W – 266433 (formerly 4168) Private William Taylor enlisted in the Hertford-shire Regiment at the county town. Whether he or his parents lived in Ware or Thundridge is not clear. He was killed in action in the lines near Festubert on the 23rd July 1916. His name is commemorated on the Thundridge War Memorial.

Whyman F – 36517 (formerly 5986) Private Frederick Whyman was a Ware man who enlisted with the Hertfordshire Regiment and was another of those transferred to the 6th Battalion Royal Berkshire Regiment. He was reported missing in action in July 1917. It was later confirmed later that he had died on the 31st July with Sergeant Joseph Newman at Glencorse Wood. His name is commemorated on the Hertford Memorial.

Williams R – 265773 Private Robert Henry Williams enlisted in the Hertfordshire Regi-ment joining the 1st Battalion in France on the 17th August 1915. It is believed that his parents came from Ware. He died of wounds received in France on the 29th April 1918. His name appears on the Thundridge War Memorial,

Walk round Ware Cemetery and you will see many of the names mentioned within this text. Many such as Sydney Presland and Richard Page MM died in the 1920s or 1930s at a relatively young age – no doubt from the effects of their wounds or from being gassed. Others like Alfred Ensby MM and William Hart lived to a ripe old age. Look carefully and you will also see the graves of the war widows and bereaved parents. Let us remember the anguish suffered by this group of people as well as those men whose lives were ruined by the ever lasting effects of gas and the pains of their wounds.

Appendix 1
The Names of the Fallen

Royal Navy
Acting Leading Stoker Harry Adams	H.M.S Maidstone
Stoker John Fensome	H.M.S Euryalus, died 1915
Leading Seaman Eric G Fitzjohn	H.M.S Commonwealth, died 1919
A.B Seaman Thomas L Gaines	H.M.S Negro, died 1916
Leading Seaman Bert Game	H.M.S Vanguard, died 1917
A.B Seaman Joseph Huckle	H.M.S Indefatigable, died 1916
Ordinary Seaman William J Lee	H.M.S Natal, died 1915
1st Class Stoker William Pearson	H.M.S Bonoventura, died 1919
A.B Seaman Percy E Smith	H.M.S Renown, died 1919

Merchant Marine   Chief Officer Horace H Albany
                                        SS Minihaha

Northumberland Hussars   Private William Brown.

Hertfordshire Yeomanry   Trooper Walter J Nickels

City of London Yeomanry   Sergeant Morris H Wilkins

Machine Gun Corps   Private Herbert P Chapman

Royal Field Artillery
Driver Walter J Acres	Capt Bernard Catling MC	Gnr William Fitzjohn
Gnr Alfred Lawrence	Gnr Arthur Storey	Driver Charles Taylor
2nd Lieut Stanley Veasey		

Royal Engineers
Sapper Cyril Lilley	L/Cpl William J May	L/Cpl Alfred H Pearce
Sapper Joseph Webb		

Grenadier Guards   Capt Alwyn Gosselin DSO   Private Walter Robertson

Coldstream Guards
	Sgt Aubrey Allen	Private Arthur V Dyson
Private Herbert Dyson	Private George Page	

Royal Scots   Private George Fensome

East Kent Regiment
Private Herbert Page	Private William J Reeves	Private Frederick Willmott

Royal Fusiliers

Private John Akers	Private William C Bignell	Private Raymond Clemo
Private Bertie Cockman		

Norfolk Regiment	Private George Davidson	
Lincolnshire Regiment	Private William J Charvill	Private Samuel Slater
Devonshire Regiment	Private George W French	

Bedfordshire Regiment

Private Reginald E Abbey	Private Albert Andrews	Capt W Gardiner Baird
Private Jonas Brett	Private William Burrell	Private Frederick Camp
Private Alban C Castle	Private Charles Catley	Private Ernest J Clare
Private Albert J Clark	Private Joseph Clark	L/Cpl Albert Clibbon +
Private William Day	Sgt Drummer William Dyer	Cpl Joseph Fitzjohn
Private Walter Game	Private William Game	Private Alfred W Gardner
Private Frederick Gladding	Sgt Herbert S Hammond	Private George A Howard
Private Charles Johnson	Private Herbert J Munt	L/Cpl George Pakes
Sgt George Presland	Sgt H G Robinson DCM	Private Amos Rogers
Private Albert W Shambrook	Private William J Shambrook	Cpl Joseph W Sibthorpe
Cpl Samuel Skinner	Private Arthur E Smith	Private James E Spencer
Private John Sweeney	Private Edwin Tidey	Private Henry Tillcock
Private Harry Trundle	L/Cpl Maurice Trundle	Private Ernest E Waller
Private John W Warwick	CSM Ernest Watson DCM	Private Ernest Watson
Private Martin F Webb		

Yorkshire Regiment	Private George W Gibbins	Private Albert Long
Lancashire Fusiliers	Private Charles W Haggar	Private George Storey
Royal Inniskilling Fusiliers	2nd Lieut. Harold A Boyd	
Gloucestershire Regiment	Private Edward A Parrott +	
Duke of Cornwall's L I	Private Frederick H Simester	
Hampshire Regiment	Private Harold W Young	
Dorsetshire Regiment	Private Edward Chittenden	
Royal Highlanders	Capt Andrew C Begg	Private Albert Trory

Essex Regiment

Private Alfred T Adams	Private John A Parnell	Private Frederick C Savage
Private William Y Wall		

Notts & Derbyshire Regt	Private George W Bardell	Private William J Wall
Loyal North Lancashires	2nd Lieut Ernest V Everard	Private Thomas D Phypers

Northamptonshire Regt

Private Peter C Bayford	Private Frederick E Dell	L/Sgt Bertram J Lawrence
Private Thomas Rousham	Private Edward Swallow MM	Private Henry Skeggs

Royal Berkshire Regt

Sgt Joseph O Newman+	Private Sidney Sargent*

Royal West Kent Regt

Private Henry Gilbey	Private Alfred W Parnell	Private Harry Vigus

Middlesex Regiment

Cpl Percy E H Allen	Private John Andrews	Private Walter W Bowcock
Private Albert F Chalkley	Private Geoffrey A Nugent	Private Charles W Smart

King's Royal Rifle Corps Rfm Harry Proctor   Sgt Andrew Wall
Wiltshire Regiment   Private Harry E Chapman Capt John R Duvall CF
Manchester Regiment   Private James Riddle   Private Henry Storey
Seaforth Highlanders   Private Henry W Pike   Private William J Wisby

Leinster Regiment

Private Edward Catley	L/Cpl James A Parsley	Private William J Sherlock

Royal Dublin Fusiliers   Private Albert Trundle

Rifle Brigade

Rfm Norman Chapman	Rfm William Ives	Rfm Frederick Mills
Cpl Archibald Norton	Rfm Henry J Wareham	

London Regiments

Private Phillip Aldridge	Private Charles J Andrews	Rfm Ernest R Bodey
Major Vincent R Hoare	L/Cpl Percy L Horning	Sgt Frank Newman DCM
Private George Trory		

1st Battalion Herts Regt

Private Charles E Adams	Private Ernest Adams	Cpl James F Akers
Private Walter Andrews	Private William Andrews	Private Charles E Cakebread
Private Ernest J Cakebread	Private Albert J Campkin*	Private Charles Castle
RSM Edward Clark MSM	Private George C Clark	Private Herbert G Clibbon
Private Joseph A Clibbon*	L/Cpl Richard Cockman MM	Private Arthur Crooks
Private Walter J French	Private Frank Gray	Private John T Gray DCM
Sgt Hiram J Hammond	Private Frederick H Hart MM	Bdsman Henry Hills
Private Percy H Huggins	L/Cpl Ernest Jackson*	Private Henry A Johnson
Private George H Keene	L/Cpl Frederick C Knight	Driver Charles Lee
Private Harry Lee	Private Charles Martin	Private Ernest Martin

A/Sgt Thomas F Martin
Private Henry C Parnell
Private Thomas H Prior
Private Charles H Salmons
Private William Shadbolt
Private Albert E Smith
Private Edward G Smith
Private Joseph Suckling
Private James Trundle
Private Frederick Whyman*

Sgt Harold D Newton
Private George Presland
Sgt George A Reynolds
Sgt Inst Thomas Saunders
Cpl James A Skinner*
Private Albert E Smith
Private William H Smith
Private Claud Sweeney MM
Sgt James Walsingham
Act SM Arthur Wilbourne

Private John G Newton
Private John Presland
Private Phillip Robinson
L/Cpl Francis Savage
L/Cpl Ernest Skipp
Private Alfred Smith*
Cpl Joseph Stamp
Private William Taylor*
Private Ernest W Warby
Private Robert Williams*

Army Service Corps
Private Stephen Graham

Private Harry J Pearce

Private Thomas Player

Army Medical Corps
QMS Alfred Badcock
Private John J Dewbury

Private Reginald T Blighty

Private Albert W Chapman

Military Mounted Police   L/Cpl Daniel Chapman   Sgt Francis H Pearce

Royal Defence Corps   Private Frederick Brazier

Royal Air Force   Sgt Harry Goldstone   Airman Nelson Waller

Colonial Forces

Canadian Royal Highlanders Private Robert Aldridge

Canadian Light Infantry   Private James Sullivan

Wellington Infantry Battalion, New Zealand Force   Cpl H Norman Rising

*   *Name not engraved on Ware War Memorial*
+   *Enlisted in the Hertfordshire Regiment*
#   *Enlisted in Bedfordshire Regiment*
CF   *Chaplain to the Forces*

Appendix 2
"The Old Contemptibles"

	Captain	Henry Page Croft* CMG	The first Territorial Officer to achieve the rank of Brigadier General.
198	Colour Sgt	Ernest W Abbot* DCM	Discharged 17th April 1916, rejoined as WO II
204	Sergeant	Joseph Ketterer* MSM	Became the battalion's RQMS.
208	Colour Sgt	W E Sheppeard*	
219	L/Corporal	Edward C Clarke*	Ended war as Coy Sergeant Major.
232	Private	Frederick Cox*	Discharged 7th April 1916.
235	Drummer	William C Hart*	Discharged 7th April 1916, rejoined and served with the King's African Rifles in East Africa as a Sergeant.
285	Private	Ernest Page*	Discharged 7th April 1916, rejoined and served in the Royal Horse Artillery and Northumberland Fusiliers, taken prisoner of war.
292	Private	William Presland*	Discharged 7th April 1916, re joined RFA, discharged through wounds 1919
319	Private	J Wood*	Discharged as L/Corporal 7 April 1915
982	L/Sergeant	William A Searle*	Discharged 14th October 1915.
1405	Private	William J H Jackson *	Wounded at Festubert.
1430	Drummer	George C Clark*	Discharged 8th March 1916, rejoined the 1st Battalion as 270491 and killed in action 3rd July 1917
1459	Private	Ernest Johnson*	Discharged 28th April 1916
1680	Private	T R Munt*	Transferred to the Royal Engineers.
1706	Drummer	William T Hills*	Wounded at Festubert in March 1918.
1707	Private	Richard W L Baldock*	
1717	Private	H Jackson*	Wounded as a Sergeant in 1918.
1814	Private	H Akers*	Transferred to 301 Labour Company, Labour Corps.
1817	Private	C Crane*	
1818	Private	Frederick W Crook*	Became CSM, Prisoner of War 1918.
1819	Private	Edward Clark* MSM	Killed as WOI (RSM) in Spring 1918.
1820	L/Corporal	Hiram J Hammond*	Promoted Sergeant, killed at St Julien.
1821	Private	Thomas F Martin*	Sergeant. killed at Third Battle of Lys.
1823	L/Corporal	John Riddle*	Wounded in 1915, promoted Sergeant.
1824	Private	Thomas E Saunders*	

1826	Private	Edward G Smith*	Killed at the Battle of Ancre.
1829	Private	Alfred Ensby* MM	Wounded at St Julien.
1832	Drummer	Leslie Delozey*	Commissioned in 6th North Stafford-shire Regiment.
1833	Private	S Goodey*	Wounded at the Battle of Ancre.
1834	Drummer	Edmund J C Parker*	
1858	Private	E W Wallace*	Wounded at Festubert, ended war in 575 Employment Company Lab Corps.
1870	Private	W Gaines* MM & Bar	Wounded as sergeant at St Julien.
2068	Private	Ben W Newton*	Transferred to 575 Employment Coy.
2069	Private	Joseph C Newton*	
2070	Private	E A Long*	Wounded and transferred to 661 Agricultural Company, Labour Corps.
2071	Private	Richard Cockman* MM	Killed on 26th April 1918.
2072	Private	Sidney A Ditton*	Wounded at Lys in 1918.
2090	Private	H W Page*	Wounded in 1918.
2108	Sergeant	Francis Rayment* DCM	Commissioned in Hertfordshire Regt.
2222	Private	H Crane*	Wounded in 1914.
2720	Private	George Presland#	Killed on 30th July 1916 while attached to the Gloucestershire Regiment.
2272	Private	Joseph A Clibbon*	Killed at the Battle of Ancre.
2276	Private	Ernest Jackson*	Killed as L/Corporal at Battle of Ancre.
2278	Private	Walter E Page*	Wounded three times.
2287	Private	Charles H Salmons*	Killed at St Julien.
2291	Private	Richard Page * MM	Wounded at St Julien.
2322	Private	J J Clark*	Probably wounded in 1916, transferred to 2nd Garrison Battalion Beds, Acting Sergeant in India.
2376	Private	A Saunders*	Wounded on the 6th February 1915, POW in 1918.
2418	Private	Albert Baker*	
2438	Drummer	Harris J*	
2510	Private	Alfred King	Transferred to the 4th Battalion Gloucester Regiment
2516	Private	Harold D Newton	Killed as Sergeant in the Gloucester Regiment 1917.
2523	Private	E G Blows #	Transferred to Machine Gun Corps.
2528	Private	Joseph A Stamp #	Rejoined the Territorials at outbreak of war, died as a Corporal at Ancre.
2547	Private	Victor Waller	Wounded at the Battle of Ancre.
2568	Private	James A Skinner #	Rejoined the Territorials at the outbreak of war, killed as a corporal at the Battle of St Julien.
2582	Private	Alfred James Bennet	Wounded with "E" Company.

2583	Private	Arthur Smith	Wounded at the Battle of Ancre, transferred to Eastern Command Labour Centre Labour Corps.
2612	Private	Albert Hawkes MC	Commissioned in Bedfordshire Regt 27th June 1917.
2636	Private	Philip J Robinson	Killed on the 19th November 1914.
2666	Private	George H Slater	Ended the war in 375 Employment Company Labour Corps.
2677	Private	Ernest Andrews	
2682	Private	Charles Castle	Accidentally killed at Le Havre 7th November 1914.
2690	Private	W E Phypers	Transferred to Essex Regt, ? from Thundridge.
2697	Private	Charles C Frost	
2701	Private	Percy H Huggins	Killed in action 25th Dec 1914
2723	Private	Alfred Baker DCM	Wounded in the German Spring offensive 1918.
2736	Private	Henry T King	Wounded in 1916, transferred to 2nd Garrison Battalion Bedfordshire Regt and served in India until 1919.
2740	Private	Henry G Campkin	Wounded at Festubert, trasnferred to 126 Labour Company.
2753	Private	Samuel Campkin	Wounded at Festubert.
2874	Private	Middleton	Wounded at the Battle of Ancre.
2865	Private	G A Reynolds MM	Killed as a sergeant at St Julien.
2869	Private	F Whitby MC and Bar	Commissioned in 19th Battalion London Regiment.
2875	Drummer	James H Cockman	Wounded 1918.
2914	Private	Harry Lee	Killed in action with 2nd Royal Berks
3287	Private	Ernest J Crook #	Pre-war Territorial who rejoined at outbreak of war., wounded in 1915 & invalided out of the Army, rejoined 2/1st Cambrigeshires.

*   *In Territorials before the war.*

\#   *Time-expired "Terrier" who rejoined the colours at the outbreak of the war. Two other pre-war Territorials – Drummer P C Jackson and Private Harry Phypers – joined the Bedfordshire Regiment.*

Appendix 3
Soldiers from Ware who joined the Hertfordshire Regiment, were transferred to other regiments and wounded in action

Regt No	Name	Address	Regiment
	Private Goldstone AV	42 Star Street	Gloucestershire Regiment
39583	Private Street E J	Bluecoat Yard	Gloucestershire Regiment
2941	Private Garner F J		Royal Berkshire Regiment
	Private Hammond H C		Royal Berkshire Regiment
	Private Barker W A	London Road	Royal Berkshire Regiment
36240	Private Bassill A	48 High Oak Road	Royal Berkshire Regiment
36244	Private Ballinger H	Star Street	Royal Berkshire Regiment
36237	Private Bently T		Royal Berkshire Regiment
36270	Private Canfield C		Royal Berkshire Regiment
36327	Private Garner W	Star Street	Royal Berkshire Regiment
36410	Private Money G		Royal Berkshire Regiment
36461	Private Muncer W	Park Road	Royal Berkshire Regiment
36419	Private Presland G	Baldock Street	Royal Berkshire Regiment
4639	Private Taylor W #		Royal Berkshire Regiment
36485	Private Timson B J	Amwell End	Royal Berkshire Regiment
	Private Warner J		Royal Berkshire Regiment
15591	Private French J	46 Bowling Rd	Royal Sussex Regiment
15643	Private Skipp T W	61 New Road	Royal Sussex Regiment
	Sgt Barrett P	58 Bowling Rd.	Royal Sussex Regiment
235256	Private King W #	Scotts Road	Lincolnshire Regiment
267028	Private French C	46 Bowling Rd	Northumberland Fusiliers
47617	Private Ernest Lee #	63 Watton Road	Northumberland Fusiliers
207097	L/Cpl Bowman L	11 Sams Yard	Royal W Surrey Regiment
203240	Private Riddle F	66 Crib Street	Yorks & Lancs Regiment
	Lieut Albert Hawkes MC	Star Street	Bedfordshire Regiment
202895	Private Blows A E	73 High Oak Road	Ox and Bucks Light Inf
6194	Private Presland J	Buryfield Terrace	Royal Fusiliers
	L/Sergeant Burton		Somerset Regiment

Prisoner of war

Appendix 4
Medals gained by Ware men who served in the Herts Regt

Companion of the Order of St Michael & St George
Major Henry Page Croft

Military Cross
Captain F Whitby MC and bar, won with the 19th London (St Pancras) Regiment
Captain Albert Hawkes MC, won with the Bedfordshire Regiment

Distinguished Conduct Medal
CSM Ernest W Abbot of Raynsford Road – King's Birthday Honours 1915
Sergeant Francis Rayment (Commissioned Lieutenant in Herts Regiment) – *ditto–*
L/Sergeant Alfred E Baker – gazetted 22nd October 1917
Private John Gray of 22 Bowling Road – won at the Battle of Ancre.
Private Herbert W Fish, attached to the 7th Battalion Bedfordshire Regiment, who also received the Russian Medal, both won in 1915. *[The Russian Medal was awarded by the Russians to the very brave. Henry Page Croft mentions in his book* Twenty Two Months Under Fire *that two Herts stretcher-bearers were sent to convey a wounded man from the trenches on the 6th February 1915. As they ran down the trench a shell knocked in the parapet and half buried the two men; both were wounded and it was suggested that they should hand over the job to others which they refused to do. Page Croft notes that both received the Russian Medal. One of the two must have been Herbert Fish]*

Military Medal & Bar
Sergeant William Gaines, 13 Vicarage Road, won at St Julien & Gauche Wood 1918

Military Medal
Lance Corporal Claud Sweeney of London Road, won at the Battle of Ancre, 1916
Sergeant George Reynolds of London Road, won at the Battle of Ancre, 1916
Private Frederick Hart of 12 Priory Street, won at the Battle of Ancre, 1916
Private (Acting Corporal) Richard Page of Bowling Road, the Battle of Ancre 1916
Private Richard Cockman, won at St Julien, 1917
L/Sergeant Alfred Ensby, won at St Julien, 1917
Private E J Marshall, won at St Julien, 1917
Sergeant George Adams, won on the 27th March 1918
Private Harry Winter

Meritorious Service Medal
CSM (A/RSM) Edward Clark – gazetted 17th June 1918 for devotion to duty
RQMS Joseph Ketterer.

Territorial Efficiency Medal
Company Regimental Sergeant Major Edward C Clarke of London Road

Medals awarded to Ware men serving with other regiments

Croix de Guerre
Private G R Baker serving with the Bedfordshire Regiment

Military Cross
Captain Bernard Catling with the Royal Field Artillery
Major Thomas Cyril Hunt with the Royal Engineers

Distinguished Service Order
Captain Alwyn Gosselin with the Grenadier Guards

Distinguished Conduct Medal
Sgt Frank Newman, 1/3rd Battalion London Regiment – Neuve Chapelle March 1915
Private Percy Pitts of "The Bungalow" Ware
Sergeant H G Robinson, Bedfordshire Regiment
Petty Officer Simpson
CSM Ernest Watson, 1st Battalion Bedfordshire Regiment – also mentioned in despatches
Private W G Baker, 18th Battalion Middlesex Regiment

Military Medal
Sapper P W Castle of New Road, 12th D S Company Royal Engineers, won in 1918
Private Francis P Howard of 91 New Road, 62 Battalion Machine Gun Corps, 1918.
Sergeant Percy Barrett of 53 Bowling Road, 4th Tank Battalion, Tank Corps, 1918
Private Horace Batstone of Church Street, 7th Battalion King's Royal Rifle Corps 1916
L/Cpl T Capel of Gladstone Road, 6th Battalion Bedfordshire Regiment 1918
Driver H W Reed with the Army Service Corps attached to Medical Corps, 1918
L/Corporal A Wallis of Vicarage Road, 9th Battalion King's Royal Rifle Corps, 1917
L/Cpl Edward Swallow with the 2nd Battalion Northamptonshire Regiment, 1916
Private Frank White of 43 Church Street, 2nd Battalion Bedfordshire Regiment, 1918
Sergeant Henry T Phypers of Thundridge, 1/1st Bn Cambridgeshire Regiment, 1918

VC for former Ware Station clerk

Although he was not a member of the Hertfordshire Regiment, a former resident of the town won the Victoria Cross in 1918. He was G58769 Lance Corporal C G Robertson MM of the Royal Fusiliers who between 1900 to 1902 was a clerk at Ware Railway Station and had served in the South African War with the Middlesex Yeomanry.

Appendix 5
Names of soldiers attending the dinner held at the Drill Hall at Amwell End on Wednesday, 29th January 1919

Chalkly J	Amwell End	Chapman W	Coronation Road
Saunders T	,,	Barker R B	,,
Timson B J*	,,	Bearman A	Crib Street
Ward A	,,	Brighty L J	,,
Chapman E	Amwell Terrace	Brinklow J	,,
Clibbon A	Baldock Street	Clifton H	,,
Clibbon C T	,,	Cockman C F	,,
Harper F	,,	Crane C *	,,
Huggins R	,,	Hills W *	,,
Presland S *#	,,	Knight A C	,,
Skeggs G*	,,	Lee F	,,
Slater G H*	,,	Moulding L	,,
Wallace J*	,,	Page A G*	,,
Boswell	Bowling Road	Shambrook J	,,
Chalkley*	,,	Skinner C	,,
Clare S H*	,,	Tillcock G	,,
Deadman C H	,,	Acres H*	Cross Street
Deadman J	,,	Riddle J*	,,
Goldstone A	,,	Slater S	,,
Watson W H	,,	Isaacs W	Fanhams Hall
Wood J*	,,	Hatherill B H *#	Garland Road
Campkin S*#	Buryfield Terrace	Sewell E	,,
Lambert A	,,	Skinner G T	,,
Presland J*	,,	Capel T MM	Gladstone Road
Dennis G A	Caroline Court	Capel W	,,
Shambrook E	,,	Crook F *#	,,
Skeggs S	,,	Taylor H A	Grasmere Road
Stamp V	,,	Taylor S A	,,
Waldo J	,,	Spencer J H	Grotto Lodge
Smith A *	Century Road	Bassill A*	High Oak Road
Goody T	Cherry Tree Yard	Blows A E*#	,,
Newton B W*	,,	Day G*#	,,
Chapman C	Church Street	Fothergill J	,,
Chapman F R	,,	Hale I	,,
Wall A H	,,	Tillcock A	,,
Smith S R	Clement Street	Wells J	,,
Adams A	Collet Road	Willmott A J	,,
Welch W	,,	Clarke S E	High Street
Parker E J C*	Coronation Road	Parrot P	,,

Prior J	High Street	Muncer V	Priory Street
Waller O*	"	Murkin A C	Raynsford Road
Dixon A J	Jeffries Road	Clarke J E	Red House Road
Clark W	Kibes Lane	Nicholson F	Round House
Cockman A	"	King A*	Scotts Road
Cockman H*	"	Timson J	Station Road
Godfrey G F	"	Ballinger W*	Star Street
Hitch E*	"	Burgess A	"
Hulls A	"	Chapman C	"
Preston H*	"	Gardner W*	"
Preston S W*	"	Gaylor F*	"
Smith W F	"	Middleton H J	"
Hammond J	King Edward's Road	Saunders A*#	"
Abbot J J	London Road	Skipp B	"
Pepper H	"	Storey J	"
Clare B	Milton Road	Deville W	The Bourne
Bardell J	Mount Street	Powell T	"
Nichols J	"	Smith A	The Pound
Adams J (Trotter)#	Musley Hill	Phillips W	The Weir
Baker A J*	"	Canfield T*	Thundridge
Cadmore W	"	Baker A L*	Trinity Road
Chapman C	"	Bolton W H	"
Head E	"	Goldstone J	"
Munt	"	Halfhide A	"
Overhill J	"	Burgess L	Vicarage Road
Storey H J	"	Burgess R	"
Tillcock S	"	Munt G	"
Winter J*	"	Pomfret D H	"
Arnall L	Musley Villas	Sams W	"
Blackmore C	New Road	Sherwood J	"
Castle P W MM	"	Titmarsh C J	"
Castle R*	"	Titmarsh J	"
Phypers H*	"	Mumford A	Ware Park Dairy
Skipp S	"	Kemsley S	Ware Union
Waller A M	"	Warner H*	Warner Road
Witney A F C	"	Chesher C	Watton Road
Andrews W	Poles Lodge	Cockman W	"
Bridges F W	Princes Street	Cooper C	"
Chapman F	Princes Street	Dorrington F	"
Clare J	"	Johnson E*	"
Martin G	"	Smith H	"
Castle C H	Priory Street	Crane A	West Street
Cook H	"	Crane E	"
Cordwell F G	Priory Street	Fish C W	"
Cordwell W	"		
Grove C	"		
Hart B J	"		
Huttlestone F	"		

*   Served with the Hertfordshire Regiment
#   Prisoner of War

Appendix 6
Sources of information and illustrations

Ware Museum
  Photographs and postcards
  Henry Page Croft's book *Twenty Two Months Under Fire*
  Frank Newman's plaque, medal and certificate

Hertfordshire Records Office
  Microfilms of the *Hertfordshire Mercury, The Mid Week Mercury* and the
  Hertfordshire Countryside magazine
  Soldiers Who Died in the War HMSO Vol 77
  Transcript of 1st Battalion's War Diary
  Manuscript of an unpublished book by the late Lieut-Col B J Gripper
  Correspondence files of the 1st Battalion Hertfordshire Regiment

Hertfordshire Library Service
  Edmund Blunden's book *Overtones of War*

Imperial War Museum, Duxford
  Medal citations and Regimental History

Public Records Office at Kew
  Medal Rolls and shipping details

Commonwealth War Graves Commission
  Details of burials

Mrs Ann Bridges	Photographs, medals and documents
Mrs Doris Copps and	Photographs, documents and information about
** Mrs Rosemary Page**	William Presland
Mrs Doris Gilbey	Information and photographs of Ernest Page
Mrs Jean Gilby	Information and photographs of the Newton family
Mr Peter King	Photographs, photography, medals and documents
Mrs Grace Knight	Photographs and memorabilia of Joseph Clibbon.
Mrs Victoria Shaw	Information on the Hart family of Priory Street
Mr David Perman	Maps of battles in which the Herts Guards fought.